THE BUSINESS TRANSITION COACH

THE BUSINESS TRANSITION COACH

Your guide to succession planning, exit strategies, and preparing for the big handoff

Wayne Vanwyck

Self-Counsel Press
(a division of)
International Self-Counsel Press Ltd.
Canada   USA

Self-Counsel Press acknowledges the financial support of the Government of Canada through the Canada Book Fund (CBF) for our publishing activities. Canada

Printed in Canada.

First edition: 2020

Library and Archives Canada Cataloguing in Publication

Title: The business transition coach : your guide to succession planning, exit strategies, and preparing for the big handoff / Wayne Vanwyck.

Names: Vanwyck, Wayne, author.

Series: Self-Counsel business series.

Description: First edition. | Series statement: Business series

Identifiers: Canadiana (print) 20200288911 | Canadiana (ebook) 20200288954 | ISBN 9781770403291 (softcover) | ISBN 9781770405127 (EPUB) | ISBN 9781770405134 (Kindle)

Subjects: LCSH: Business planning. | LCSH: Family-owned business enterprises—Succession. | LCSH: Executive succession—Planning. | LCSH: Industrial management. | LCSH: Retirement—Planning.

Classification: LCC HD30.28 .V36 2020 | DDC 658.4/012—dc23

Self-Counsel Press
(a division of)
International Self-Counsel Press Ltd.

| North Vancouver, BC | Bellingham, WA |
| Canada | USA |

CONTENTS

PREFACE   xi

INTRODUCTION   xv

1 PLAN FOR TRANSITION   1
   1. The Financial Benefit   5
   2. The Motivation to Sell   7
   3. Fear of the Dreaded Phone Call   8
   4. If You Don't Make a Plan   10

2 GET YOUR LIFE ON A ROLL   14
   1. Redefine Retirement   14
   2. How Do You Define Success?   15
   3. The Value of Written Goals   18
   4. Getting Started with Goal Setting   20
   5. Business Transition Reality Check   30

3 TRANSITION MEANS CHANGE   32
   1. Change Is Constant   32

2. Complacency: The Killer of Necessary Change   33

3. Boiling a Frog   34

4. Why Do Most Entrepreneurs Fail to Plan
for the Inevitable?   36

5. Deciding Is Not Enough   37

6. The Eight Steps of the Change Process   38

7. Change Requires Leadership   41

4 CHOOSE YOUR BEST OPTION FOR TRANSITION   42

1. Option 1: Preparing to Sell   43

2. Option 2: Work Hard until You Die or Become Disabled   52

3. Option 3: Burn out and Sell to the First Buyer   54

4. Option 4: Wind down the Business and Close It   55

5. Option 5: Keep the Business   57

5 GET YOUR BUSINESS READY FOR TRANSITION   60

1. Turn Good Intentions into Action   60

2. Take Stock: Where Are You Now?   61

3. How to Estimate the Value of Your Business   61

4. Factors Affecting the Valuation of Your Business   64

5. How to Define Your Transition Goal   65

6. The Benefits of Reaching Your Goal   67

7. Considering the Challenges and Obstacles   68

8. Action Steps: Things to Do, with Timelines   70

9. Is It Worth It?   71

6 BUILD AN "A" TEAM OF ADVISORS   73

1. Selling a Business Is Not a DIY Program:
Find an Advisor   73

2. Putting Together Your "A" Team of Advisors   79

3. Ten Tests for Finding a Trustworthy Advisor   81

7 WORK ON THE BUSINESS, NOT IN THE BUSINESS   82

1. Can You Do More "Leading" Activities and
Fewer "Doing" Activities?   85

    2. Time 86

    3. Start the Change Process 91

8 EFFECTIVE DELEGATION 93

    1. Your Job Description 94

    2. What the Business Needs 95

    3. An Individual or a Team? 96

    4. Benefits and Challenges of Effective Delegation 96

    5. An Implied Contract 99

    6. Consequences of Not Delegating Effectively 100

    7. How Much Authority? 100

    8. Who's Responsible for the End Result? 102

    9. Delegation Is Key to Business Success 104

9 CREATE A BUSINESS PLAN FOR TRANSITION 105

    1. Where Are You Going? 105

    2. Hire a Facilitator 107

    3. What Do You Want? 108

    4. A More Nuanced Look at Succession Planning 110

    5. Practices 116

10 LEVERAGE YOUR ASSETS IN SUCCESSION PLANNING 117

    1. Your Most Important Asset: People 117

    2. What's Happening in Your Company? 124

    3. The Right People 126

    4. Performance Training 127

    5. Great People Management 129

    6. Visionary Leadership 130

    7. Business Diagnostics 130

11 SUCCESS IS A PROCESS 133

    1. Where Should You Start? 135

12 TEST THE WATERS WITH A SABBATICAL 148

    1. Take a Sabbatical or Long Vacation 148

2. The Goal   150

3. New Possibilities   154

4. The Bucket List   154

5. Time off Is Good for Your Business   155

6. Yeah, But ...   156

DOWNLOAD KIT   158

SAMPLE

1 The Last Un-Will and Testament   13

TABLES

1 US Businesses for Sale and How Many Actually Sell   xvi

2 Cashflow Quadrant   57

3 Working on or in the Business   83

4 Now versus Transition   87

5 Levels of Authority   103

6 Types of Employees   119

NOTICE TO READERS

PREFACE

If you are a business owner, chances are seven in ten that you are thinking about selling your business but have little or no idea how to do it.

Several years ago, a friend's brother whom I'll call Franklin decided to sell his business. He had grown a very successful industrial supply distribution company. He was doing about $10 million in profitable sales, was a pillar of the business community, and was liked by his employees. To all appearances, he was a very successful business owner.

With some fanfare, Franklin announced to his family that he and his wife were going to sell the business and retire in five years. Many who knew his workaholic ways raised their eyebrows in disbelief. He didn't have any outside hobbies and thought about the business 24/7. He despised vacations and when his wife insisted, he would grudgingly go along (looking for business opportunities along the way). No one could see him walking away from his business without a struggle. Sure enough, although his wife retired right on time, the date for Franklin's planned departure came and went.

Unfortunately, his plan wasn't really a plan. It was barely a good intention. Perhaps it was just a ruse to placate his spouse.

As his deadline approached, he threw a monkey wrench into the business, creating a huge challenge that only he could solve. He changed his major supplier after selling the same product line for more than 20 years. To this day, no one knows for sure why he did it, but the consequences were catastrophic. Clients left. Salespeople quit. His business went into a tailspin. Of course, Franklin nobly renounced his intention to retire. Now he could swoop in like Superman to save the day.

Unfortunately, the crisis he created was bigger than he anticipated and things continued to deteriorate. He was under far more stress than ever in his business career. Within a couple of years, he was in danger of losing everything.

His sister, a business consultant, offered to relocate several hundred miles to help him. She ended up running the company because he was so emotionally and physically stressed that he was institutionalized and put on medication to prevent him from committing suicide. He was literally banging his head against the wall.

In the end, he did sell his business for cents on the dollar but the experience was devastating. Franklin's opportunity to retire with wealth and a stellar reputation turned into a nightmare that reduced him to a shadow of his former self. He lost the respect of his employees, his customers, and his family. He lost millions of dollars. He no longer speaks to his sister, with whom he had previously been very close.

If only someone had said to him when he announced his intention to retire in five years, "Let's get started! Here's a step-by-step process that will ensure that you're ready in that time," he could have saved himself incalculable grief. But as I looked around, it became obvious to me that no such program or process existed. Sure, there were books that told you how to value your business or how to negotiate the best price. But there was nothing on how to get mentally, emotionally, and practically prepared for the day when you sell or step away from your business.

Maybe this is an extreme example, but in speaking with hundreds of business owners about this, one thing has become clear. It's a very difficult step to sell a business. It's an amazingly complex and foreign process. It's a lot of work. Business owners don't have a lot of time to do it. And their businesses are their babies ... things they have created, nurtured, grown, defended, and loved for many years. Giving them up threatens to leave enormous holes in their lives.

That's the reason for this book. My humble goal is to alert you to the coming sell-off of businesses as aging entrepreneurs sell and retire in record numbers. If you start planning your transition before it becomes urgent or you have no choice, you can profit greatly. You will be better able to sell your business or put it into family or employee hands in a way that maximizes value for all concerned.

You don't have to be like Franklin, undoing a lifetime of solid, creative work by not being ready for the next stage in your life and the life of your business.

I've struggled myself with this issue. As a serial entrepreneur, I've found it fun and exciting to start businesses but difficult to give them up. I've written this book for all of us who are struggling with the questions of what to do next, how to let go, and how to get the most value from our years of blood, sweat, and tears.

INTRODUCTION

This is urgent. I don't know about you, but I am bothered by some statistics. I'll be sharing numbers throughout this book, for example, as of this writing 70 percent of entrepreneurs intend to retire in the next few years but very few of those entrepreneurs have a written plan for succession (PWC, www.pwc.com/ca/en/private-company/once-in-a-lifetime.html, accessed March, 2020).

That's a tsunami of change, a wave of literally millions of businesses owned by wannabe retirees who don't have a transition plan. This doesn't even include those who may die or become disabled in the same time frame. This is a massive liability for the economy and for business owners who don't know where to turn.

This is a source of deep insecurity for employees who may have a lifetime of service invested in these companies. Conversely, it's a huge opportunity for those with the ability to purchase businesses.

Following in Table 1 is another interesting set of statistics, from the book *Successfully Sell Your Business* (Rogerson Business Services, 2011).

This means that the majority of businesses have less than a 20 percent chance of selling when put on the market. These facts raise some disturbing questions in my mind:

Table 1
US Businesses for Sale and How Many Actually Sell

Number of Employees	Percentage of All Businesses	Number that Sell
< 10	80%	1 in 5.5
10–20	9%	1 in 4
21–100	8%	1 in 3.5
> 100	3%	1 in 3

- What happens to a business, its employees, and its suppliers when the owner decides to sell but hasn't planned for it?

- What happens to the owners when they are unable to sell their businesses for what they think they're worth, or when they are unable to sell them at all?

- What resources are out there to help owners maximize business value and prepare to sell in order to get the dollars they want in return for their years of toil and risk?

- What will happen to the economy when millions of businesses come up for sale? Who's going to buy all those businesses?

- If only a small percentage of businesses that go up for sale are actually sold, what happens to all the others? What happens to the owners, the clients, the employees, the suppliers?

- If there are millions of businesses for sale, how does an individual owner make his or her business stand out and be attractive to prospective buyers so it is more likely to be one that is chosen?

- Is there a step-by-step formula for success in selling a business that could help an entrepreneur avoid many of the pitfalls and losses while leveraging his or her company to increase its value?

- Why do so few business owners have a plan and how can we help them to prepare so they sell their businesses on purpose instead of by default?

- What options do business owners have if they don't want to sell their businesses but do want to slow down?

This book is for entrepreneurs (and their families) who have built their own companies and are considering transition. That transition can take many forms, from simply slowing down or developing an Employee Share Ownership Plan (ESOP) to engaging a partner or selling the business outright.

Let me define some terms. Succession planning is often used to describe the process of creating and executing a strategy for a business so no one individual can make it vulnerable if the owner were to quit, die, or become disabled. Proper succession planning ensures that there are people in the wings ready to take over should such a tragedy occur. This should apply to the owner of the company as well as to key players whose absences would jeopardize the smooth running of the organization. We'll use the term succession planning for the process of putting the right people in the right roles and developing a system of training, mentoring, and preparing others to take over at some time in the future.

While succession planning will be part of our discussion, our primary focus is transition planning. I'm going to use this term to describe the process of changing your role as the owner-manager of the business to something else. The end result of transition planning could be:

- You sell or give your business to family members.

- You sell to an employee, a group of employees, or a competitor.

- You sell to an investment group or a public corporation.

- You merge with another company.

- You continue to run your business for many more years. Then you choose to evolve your role so that you have less responsibility, less stress, and fewer hours. Or you choose to work just as hard, but in a more strategic rather than hands-on role. Either way, you can make sure your business is in prime shape to sell if you ever have to do so.

- You choose to wind down your business and close it.

Both transition planning and succession planning are crucial and urgent activities for the world's aging population of business owners. The situation will be a crisis for many businesses unless it is dealt with effectively in the very near future. That said, most of this book is valuable reading for any entrepreneur. All businesses will benefit from implementing the ideas and strategies shared here.

This book will alert you to the issues that stand between you and a successful transition. You will visualize your ideal lifestyle, strategize, and set goals for the successful execution of your plan, and learn how to avoid many of the mistakes suffered by others. Most importantly: You will take action on the plan starting immediately.

The purpose of this book is to get you to —

- make time to think ahead;

- recognize and deal with the inevitable;

- plan for your personal transition;

- prepare for the transition of your company; and

- begin to execute that plan now, even if you think you are years from making the change.

Let me introduce the peers whom I interviewed for this book; some reappear in the pages to follow, and all of them have contributed to my thinking (names have been changed to ensure the privacy of those who have shared their stories):

- Mark sold his construction business and made enough money so his children and grandchildren will never have to work. Recently, he and a few friends got together and decided to start a bank. However, the sale of his business made him emotionally, mentally, and physically ill for more than a year.

- Lori was a sole proprietor. She was approached by a complementary business and completed the sale of her business in five months. She continues to work for the new owner and is happier being an employee.

- Don sold his service business but continued to work for the firm that bought him out. It was hell. He couldn't wait for his contract to end so he could retire and spend time with his wife traveling North America in a new RV.

- Greig sold his medical devices business and is now working overseas for Habitat for Humanity. He has never been happier.

- Rob sold part of his business to a partner and continues to invest in it because he sees tremendous growth potential and a social mission that he can advance. But, he now spends most of his time traveling.

- Bill sold his business, then continued to work as a consultant for the new owner to evaluate and buy other businesses that would complement the product line.

- Scott sold his business but arranged to maintain control until all the money was paid. The first buyer didn't pay in full, so Scott took it back and sold it again for considerably more money. Sadly, in the process he lost his wife and his kids.

- Tom thought his son might take over the business and waited until he was 70 to learn that his son wasn't really interested. Tom wound it down, gave the furniture away, and turned out the lights.

- Arun always said he would retire at 60. Five years before he hit that milestone, he confirmed the decision with his team. Working with his advisors and his senior management, he developed a systematic, time-bound action plan for building the capabilities of his team and maximizing the competitiveness of his business. Arun sold his business at a price that was a pleasant surprise even to his own team. Now he leads a quiet but active life with his wife on their horse farm.

I conducted interviews with these and many other individuals from Texas to Newfoundland. Some of the stories are sad. Some of the people I spoke to did not prepare properly. They didn't get the right advice. They didn't take the time necessary to think it through. As a result, they left money on the table, got sucked back into the business, or committed to a painful process that could have been avoided.

Many others did prepare properly. Some owners got a lot of money in return for their long years of sweat equity and willingness to risk what they had for the future. They travel. They volunteer. They spend time with their families. They mentor others. They start up new enterprises.

You may be thinking that it's easier to start a business than to sell one. You're probably right. But when you started out, you had a vision of what you wanted, where you were going, and how you were going to get there. We now have to chart some new waters, but making a successful transition will involve going through many of these same processes. Throughout this book we will outline a map of the territory that lies ahead for you. You will —

- develop a vision of where you want to be personally;

- develop a vision of where you want the business to be and how your personal and business visions align or conflict;

- take stock of where you are now;

- set personal goals;

- set strategic goals for the business;

- assess the financial reality and what you require to achieve your goals;

- get buy-in from those who will contribute to or participate in the end results;

- gather advisors who can guide you through uncharted territory and give you critical information that will maximize your business value, minimize your taxes, and help you develop plans to get you where you want to go;

- build a list of tasks and activities that need to be undertaken; and

- follow through on and execute those tasks.

As you can imagine, this is not something you can do in a two-day workshop or on a whim — not if you want to leverage and receive the greatest value for the years of blood, sweat, and tears you have invested in your business. It's a shame to see people work hard all their lives and then give up hundreds of thousands — maybe even millions — of dollars, simply because they didn't invest the time and energy in this end stage of their businesses.

That's not to say that what you need to learn is rocket science or even new to you. But it will take on a different focus. While you already know about goal setting, leadership, and delegation, you'll be guided in examining these topics from the perspective of preparing your business for transition or sale. This means that you're going to think about them differently. You're going to ask yourself and others different questions. You're going to develop new insights regarding topics that you may not have considered before. You're going to set a date, which will increase your sense of urgency.

As the owner of this book, you will have access to a number of tools:

1. **Online forms and checklists:** This book contains forms and checklists for you to reflect upon, act upon, and complete. You can do so with pen and paper or on your computer. It's up to you. The forms are available online at the URL printed at the back of the book.

2. **Goal setting:** Goal setting is a key component of this process. Don't worry; this book makes it fun. The whole point is for you to know what you want and to go after it in a progressive, disciplined way. This book supports you as you develop some long-, mid-, and short-term goals. You may need to step outside your comfort zone. As a business owner, you've been doing that all your life. For some, preparing to transition away from a business is the toughest challenge yet. For others, it's a wonderful adventure. This process ensures that it's more likely to be the latter for you than the former.

3. **References and resources:** You will find a number of internet addresses, book recommendations, and additional resources that you can delve into in order to expand your knowledge and understanding. Now, let's get started on your unique and life-changing journey.

1
PLAN FOR TRANSITION

Here's a story about letting go.

"Good afternoon, folks. I'm Ralph Thornton speaking to you from sunny Atlanta and I'm here with sportscaster and former Olympic track athlete Bill Nichols reporting on the 1,000-meter relay. The four teams are already running and right now John King from ACME Group is in the lead. He has run an amazing first leg of the race and is at least two strides ahead of the next runner from XYZ Corp.

"King is closing the gap on his team member Les Prince, who you can see is champing at the bit to go. Closer, closer, and there's the handoff! Prince has it now, but wait, wait, King is still hanging on! Sweat is dripping from him and his hands must be slippery. He's now holding on with both hands! I've never seen anything like it before! Prince is looking confused and uncertain but he's trying to pull the baton away. They're arguing and wait, you can see the other three runners are pulling ahead, looking back with big grins on their faces.

"Oh no! What is this? Bill, have you ever seen anything like this before? King has now taken back the baton and he's beating Prince with it! Whacking him about the head! Prince is down with blood pouring from his wounds and King is running again! He's at least a half a lap behind the others, he's obviously exhausted, yet he's trying to catch up!"

"Yes Ralph, I have seen this before, and tragically, it's not as rare as you might think. We see a lot of this in the minors. King is displaying an insidious disease called "incompacete-hangerongus," the inability to let go. Unfortunately, he's failed the team and himself. He's just cost ACME the race and at the same time he's lost his reputation, his pride, and millions in future sponsorships. It's a terrible shame. He worked so hard to get to this point. If only he'd spoken up earlier, his coaches could have cured him before this race."

Some entrepreneurs find it painful to plan for transition and follow through on that plan. They founded the business and regardless of how much it has expanded or changed, it is still their baby. They imagined it, created it, nurtured it through tough times, and proudly watched it grow. They are intimately connected with its daily ebb and flow. They can't imagine what they would do if they couldn't continue to lead the organization.

Why should you plan for your transition? Because it is your responsibility to do so and you are the only one who can.

Transition will occur regardless of whether it is planned or not.

If you don't deal with succession and transition for your business, who the heck do you think will?

Some owners take the coward's way out. Perhaps at a subconscious level they hope they'll die before they have to deal with their transition. It's such a foreign, threatening process that they don't know where to start.

I've interviewed and worked with many former business owners. When I asked how they felt just before selling, I heard, "I was terrified," "I sweated bullets, " and "I was scared to death" from individuals who had courageously built very successful enterprises. Oddly enough, when I asked how they felt afterward, I heard, "I felt relieved, " "I felt a tremendous weight drop off my shoulders, " and "I felt at peace."

In other words, the anxiety and fear was much worse than the real thing and ultimately the payoff was worth the effort. One owner confided that when he couldn't get around the store to meet his customers and staff without being pushed in a wheelchair, he knew it was time to make the move. Once he had done so, he admitted he should have sold his business years earlier. He learned that he liked being retired.

Planning for transition is definitely one of the most important things you can do for your business. Why?

- It puts a strategic plan in place for the next stage of the business.

- It enables talented employees to step forward, grow, and take on more responsibility.

- It increases the value of the business by replacing you, the founding entrepreneur, with a team that can manage, instead of leaving the business vulnerable by having all of its eggs in your basket.

- It can be invigorating for you, leading to a new and exciting chapter in your life.

- Loyal family members or existing leaders may be rewarded with more responsibility. This prevents them from leaving because it is taking too long or they have no definite timeline. (Think how long Prince Charles has been on the sidelines.)

- It creates greater stability and retention of key employees in the business when employees know what to expect and how things will evolve.

- It prepares and positions the business to be sold at the right time for the right price for the least amount of taxes and minimal business disruption.

- It enables you to set up a secure income outside the business that is not vulnerable to downturns or your diminished capacity.

- It makes suppliers and clients feel more secure, which means they're less likely to transfer to competitors.

In addition to all of these benefits, the stakeholders in the business as a whole benefit when you take the responsibility to guide the transition process to its optimal conclusion. To not do so is foolish, thoughtless, and destructive — not the kind of legacy you want to leave.

Gord was finally ready to sell his business. He'd had enough. He was 63 and felt time ticking away. Not only had his children grown up while he was working, but now his grandchildren were also missing his attention.

The truth was, Gord was exhausted. By the time he finished his normal ten-hour day, he just didn't have any energy left to play with his grandchildren. Even his weekends were taken up with work that he couldn't seem to get done otherwise.

He had thought about selling his business on many occasions, but he liked his printing operation. He had started it 33 years earlier and it was his baby. He waffled between his desire to let it go and his need to hang on. That and the day-to-day momentum of old habits were powerful currents. The thought of quitting was like paddling upstream.

Was it irresponsible to quit or not to quit? Was selling the business really quitting? Conflicting emotions paralyzed him. As a result, he never got past the thinking-about-it stage.

In the quiet moments of a Sunday morning when his wife was off to church and he had the house to himself, flashes of insight made him acutely aware that he had to do something. It was his business. He ran it. It was his responsibility. If he didn't take charge of the situation, no one else would.

Then doubts would flood in. "What do I tell my employees? Will they be able to carry it on? Who will buy this business? What's it worth? Is it worth anything without me there to run it? If I tell my suppliers, will they stop giving me credit? Will the bank pull my line of credit?"

The questions didn't end there. "Will my managers start looking for other jobs? Will my customers start dealing with that new place around the corner? Who knows anything about selling a business and what will their advice cost? My lawyer has been on my case for a couple of years to get started on this. I'm sure he's licking his chops at the fees involved. What about taxes? What about my kids and their interests? What will I do if I'm not working? What about … "

The complexity and enormity of the change seemed overwhelming. With a shake of his head, he would return to reading the news, effectively shutting down the logical side of his brain that knew he had a problem.

Gord attended one of my seminars and I spoke to him afterwards about his situation. After explaining what was going on, he told me he was planning to call me about this soon.

One morning a couple months later, he rolled out of bed, started toward the washroom, and collapsed on the floor. He had suffered a debilitating stroke. He couldn't speak. He couldn't move. He could still think, though, and one can only imagine the things that were going through his mind as his wife called 911 and he was taken away in the ambulance. Unfortunately, no one will ever know for sure what he was thinking, because Gord died a week later without regaining his ability to communicate.

As a typical tough entrepreneur, you're probably thinking, "Yes, that could happen to others, but it won't happen to me." Well, I've got some bad news for you: It can happen at any time, at any place, when it's least expected. By all means, hope for the best and expect the best, but plan for the worst, just in case.

1. The Financial Benefit

Think of it this way: Suppose for the moment that you had the time and the opportunity to spend 36 months or more to prepare to sell your business. Imagine that you took a deliberate action every month to move toward its sale or transition. One month, you might speak with your accountant, lawyer, business coach, financial advisor, or banker. Another month, you might meet with your management team and talk about the future. Another month, you might work on cleaning up your inventory and freshening up your facilities. Still another month, you could get started on gathering your employees' experience and historical knowledge about company systems, complete with binders that detail every step of each process.

With all other things being equal — the market, your product cycle, the economy — can you see how a thoughtful, planned approach to systematically preparing your business for transition will make it go so much more smoothly? Can you see how taking these steps will help you sell all or some of your shares for more money?

Scott in Fort Meyers sold his company for millions and shared that he got a much higher multiple for his business than anyone else he knew in his industry.

"It was because of the systems we had in place," he said. "When the prospective buyer walked into my office and saw the bookcase filled with binders that detailed every aspect of the business, he was impressed. We detailed how the receptionist would answer the phone, how we went through the screening and hiring process, how bonuses were structured, how the bathrooms were cleaned, and what we would do if our profit margins ever dropped below a certain number.

"And we were very profitable! But what really impressed him was that he saw that our people followed the system. It wasn't just a nice platitude and fancy words on a page; we did what we said we should do. We got almost seven times earnings in an industry that averaged about three and a half to four."

> Because he had created a business with systems underpinning it, Scott was able to double the value he received when he sold. As a result, he was also able to share the wealth. He gave more than $3 million to employees to show his appreciation for their part in a highly successful transaction.

Similar results could be yours if you begin to make the time to methodically prepare your business for sale over the next three years.

Now take a moment to imagine continuing to run it as you have over the past three years and then having to sell one day because of disability, death, or some other catastrophe. This exercise brings up several important points.

- You can take various steps to improve the salability, attractiveness, and value of your business.

- Good luck has been defined as the place where preparedness meets opportunity. You should always be prepared to sell, because you never know when the right opportunity will present itself. You might get lucky.

- You know from experience that setting a goal with a clear deadline works better than not crystallizing your plan. Saying that you'll sell the business "someday" is just a weak-kneed intention. It might happen — or it might not.

- If you believe in the law of attraction — that setting a clear goal with a firm deadline can attract opportunities that otherwise wouldn't surface — then it is important to let the "universe" know what you want.

- It is not much of a stretch to believe that good planning and focused attention can increase the value of your business by 25 percent or more. Try getting that return on your investment portfolio! On the other hand, it isn't much of a stretch to think that if you had to sell at an inopportune time because of the myriad of things that could go wrong in your business, you could lose 25 percent or more of the value of your business.

On that last point, consider this graphic example: Suppose when your financial advisor asks you what you believe your business is worth so he can consider it as part of your retirement plan, you tell him $2 million. You may or may not be right, but let's say that you are. If you could increase the value by 25 percent over the next 36 months by acting on the suggestions in this book, perhaps investing ten hours per month, your value increases to $2.5 million. Not bad!

However, if three years from now you haven't done anything differently, and you have to sell because a disability is preventing you from running it anymore, or your market has gone in the toilet, your business could easily lose 25 percent or more in value, dropping to $1.5 million.

So the difference isn't just 25 percent, it's an easy 50 percent. On a $2 million company, the planning and actions you take over the next three years could be worth $1 million! A million dollars divided into 360 hours of effort is $2,777 per hour or $27,777 per month. Can you think of a more profitable way to spend your time?

2. The Motivation to Sell

I ask people who have sold their businesses this question: "When you sold your business, were you moving away from your business or toward something else?" It's an important question because it speaks to their motivations. It provides insight into what they might be doing next. It also indicates how they feel about their businesses.

Pose that question to yourself: When you do transition or sell your business, will you be pushing away from it or will you be attracted toward something else — a new goal, a new hobby, a new career, something you've always dreamed of?

If you are simply moving away from the business, what do you plan to do when you get away?

One of the biggest fears of entrepreneurs who have built a business over the years and put their heart and soul into it is, "What will I do if I don't have my business?" For many, they are their business and their business is them. They are inseparable. Their personality, persona, and self-image are intricately tied to the enterprise. They aren't okay with just being "John Smith." They are "John Smith, the owner and founder of ABC Company." They are the active member of the industry association, the Chamber of Commerce, and the buyers' group, and a friend to suppliers, customers, and employees. Their lives revolve around their positions as successful business owners.

While many business owners intend to sell their business sometime in the next five years, few have a plan. They really haven't thought about it. They're so busy running things and pondering how to make the business better, they feel they have little time to reflect on their own future. That's unfortunate, because by not making the time to plan the future, they may never set in motion the steps required for them to get what they want.

So when the time comes to transition from your business, will you be moving away from it or toward something else? Will you wake up one day and announce that you've had enough? Will you be frightened by all the possible "What ifs?"

One successful entrepreneur told me, "I had no idea how big a hole it would leave in my life when I sold my business. Every Wednesday morning I had an association meeting that I wasn't invited to anymore. The suppliers I joked with, the customers who looked forward to seeing me, the employees who worked their butts off for me — all that was gone. It took me two years to get over that feeling of loss."

3. Fear of the Dreaded Phone Call

"What motivated you to sell your business when you did?" I asked Tom.

"You'll understand this when I say it," he replied. "The fear of the dreaded phone call – the factory blew up. Someone was killed or maimed by some of the dangerous equipment we run. The vice president quit. The employees are unionizing. You know. Those things that could go wrong that would fundamentally and dramatically change everything."

Entrepreneurs often feel like they're playing the midway arcade game in which they have to whack all the gophers that keep popping back up. They try to handle the above issues with insurance, safety policies, positive employee practices, training, and regular communications with key people. But when I talked with Tom about selling his business, I perceived that somewhere along the way, the gophers had grown in number.

Dino was in year four of a five-year track to sell his business when he received an offer.

"Why did you sell?" I asked him.

"The offer wasn't what I was looking for, but I was afraid the market might drop and the business could be worth less a year later," he said.

As it turned out, his fear was justified. Shortly after he sold, the market tanked. If he hadn't sold, he could have lost 50 percent of the value almost overnight. Because he had been 80 percent through a planned approach when the offer came in, he was in a good position to recognize that the time was right and make his move.

Why are we motivated to act? Either to gain a benefit or avoid a loss. The majority of the business owners I interviewed sold to avoid a loss.

In some cases, fear had become a stronger force in their life than their former optimism, confidence, and strength. They wanted to sell before it was too late; before something that they couldn't fix went wrong; before their company lost value; before their health declined.

In some cases, the fear was healthy. Things can and do go wrong. If entrepreneurs stop doing the things that made the business successful, or if they lose their spark, they should either sell before the business slides backwards or pull themselves up by their bootstraps and get back on track.

The problem with selling when you are acting from a state of fear or pessimism is that you are far more likely to make mistakes. You may truncate the process because you are uncomfortable with your feelings and want the whole thing to go away. You may accept a lower price than you should. You may fail to consider other options that could provide a better deal for you, your employees, and your family. You may be reactive instead of proactive in managing the process.

Fear tends to come from a real or perceived lack of control. The antidote for fear is confidence. If you have done your homework, watched the trends, and know that the timing is right, you can sell from a position of absolute confidence and abundance rather than of abject fear and scarcity.

Fear in itself is not always a bad thing. It can be a more powerful motivator to take action than the promise of a benefit. The key is to feel the fear, recognize it for what it is, and then do something anyway. Know what you want to achieve. Develop action steps that will move you toward what's necessary to transition the business on your terms. Your why or your motivation for taking action has to be strong enough to outweigh your fears. Business owners who have been most successful in selling their businesses have done so with a plan. They have —

- enhanced their employees, their leadership team, and their sales;

- positioned the right people in the right roles;

- strengthened their story of future potential by ensuring long-term, happy clients;

- cleaned up their balance sheet;

- developed reproducible systems and processes that were consistently followed and proven to work;

- understood their industry, their competition, and their market;

- prepared themselves emotionally for the transition; and

- watched the timing and chosen when to sell.

They were then able to set the terms of their sale with greater confidence.

If the gophers are popping up in increasing strength or numbers in your situation, confront them and use them to motivate you to shore up your defenses. Take the initiative to get your house in order sooner rather than later. Gophers don't make good long-term pets.

4. If You Don't Make a Plan

If you don't make a plan, by default you enable the government, lawyers, and your management team to take charge in the event of your premature death or disability. That might be okay, but things probably won't proceed the way you would have chosen if you had taken the time to decide. For an amusing but informative example of how this could play out, check out the Un-Will in Sample 1.

Not having a plan may also lead to a reactive approach to selling your business rather than a proactive, thoughtful, and managed approach. Because of a business situation that was becoming more difficult to manage, Marcel just about sold his service business to the wrong guy.

 Marcel had what he believed was a willing buyer who said he had the money to complete the deal. Marcel was a willing seller, and the timing seemed right. His business was just about to launch into a profitable year after investing heavily in infrastructure, marketing, and human resources.

The buyer was an employee: A senior manager with the business who had helped the company get to the point where it could progress to the next level if he managed it well.

But the deal fell apart because of this manager's lack of integrity. What Marcel heard from this man and what he saw were in conflict with each other. While the manager involved was very persuasive, Marcel gradually realized that he couldn't be trusted. In the beginning, he chalked it up to hyperbole and exaggeration.

"I thought he was eccentric. An odd duck," he said. "But discrepancies kept cropping up."

Over time, embellishment accelerated so that lies and deceptions became part of the norm and "reality" was an elusive concept.

Marcel recalled that his prospective buyer at times behaved like Jekyll and at other times like Hyde.

"He was your best friend. He was your worst nightmare. He praised his peers one day and cursed them the next. He created conflict and stress where none was required."

Marcel said the manager was brilliant and lucid at times but then deteriorated to doublespeak and gobbledygook when asked to explain a problem that was his responsibility. "Pinning him down was like trying to nail jelly to the wall."

And the prospective buyer was smart enough to salt his story with just enough verifiable facts, tempting Marcel to believe the rest. In truth, he wanted to believe.

Marcel was not so different from the rest of us. When we want something badly enough, we tend to filter the information we receive to support our goal, not necessarily the truth.

When it came down to finalizing the sale, a picture emerged that shed new light on the oddball things the manager had been doing. He had been manipulating numbers and positioning the business to be sold for a fraction of its value. He threatened to sabotage the business if he didn't get his way.

"In hindsight, there were red flags that I should have heeded earlier," Marcel said. "I kicked myself for a long time for not trusting my instincts and connecting the dots a lot sooner."

In the end, Marcel chose not to sell his business, but he could have saved himself a lot of time, hassle, and money if he had exhibited stronger critical thinking and listened to his intuition sooner. While he knew he couldn't trust the manager to always tell the truth, he thought he could at least trust him not to be malicious or crooked. But he learned what Gandhi meant when he said, "One man cannot do right in one department of life whilst he is occupied in doing wrong in any other department. Life is one indivisible whole. " In other words, if you can't trust people completely, you can't trust them at all.

Selling your business to someone you don't trust raises important issues:

- Will you actually get paid what is promised?

- Will the deal be renegotiated after you've let your guard down?

- Will the negotiations be dragged on deliberately so the value of your business drops?

- Will there be side deals going on with employees to weaken your business and your position as owner?

- Will the prospective buyer be getting confidential inside information or client data with the intent of going after your clients regardless of any nondisclosure or confidentiality agreements?

- If you can't trust some of the information you are getting from the prospective buyer, what part of the information can you trust? It's hard to discern when a liar is telling the truth.

- How will that person treat your employees once he or she has control?

- What will happen to your reputation if your name remains on the business or, worse still, you end up working for the company for a year or more on contract?

Marcel's experience reinforces a rule that I try to live by: I only do business with people I like, respect, and trust. A rule that's well worth remembering.

Sample 1 is used with permission from Jim Ruta International.

As you can see, there's a lot to do. Worksheet 1 (available on the downloadable forms kit; see the back of the book for instructions for accessing it) shows a partial list of what you need to consider in preparing your business for transition. Why plan? Because leaving these and other items to chance is a fool's way to run a business. To think otherwise is a fantasy. Might you get lucky and sell your business for as much as you think it is worth without all this work? You might. You might win a lottery, too, but don't bet your future on it. As Phillips and Jackim have put it in *The $10 Trillion Opportunity*, (Exit Planning Institute, 2006), "Business owners who make the transition out of a business involuntarily, that is, due to family responsibilities, financial difficulties, or poor health, report they have much greater difficulty adjusting to retirement. In contrast, business owners who plan for retirement and voluntarily exit their businesses are three times more likely to be satisfied with the retirement experience and adjust more successfully to the role of retiree."

Sample 1
The Last Un-Will and Testament

Your will is vital to your family security. This is a tongue-in-cheek look at what your legacy might be if you do not have a will. This is not a will. Please consult your lawyer immediately to write or update your will.

— Jim Ruta

The Last Un-Will and Testament

This is the last un-will and testament of me, _____

Believing that government bureaucrats are better suited and qualified than I am to choose an executor for my estate, I leave it to them to settle my estate in whatever fashion they find expedient and convenient for them.

I give my blessing to government bureaucrats taking as long as possible to handle my estate without any regard whatsoever for the financial, emotional or material needs of my surviving family.

Not wanting to upset anyone or cause any hard feelings during my lifetime, I direct that government bureaucrats arbitrarily choose guardians for my minor children without due regard for my wishes or theirs. Instead, the Court can be swayed by expediency and legal power. Even though they would have no parents in this event, my children need not be consulted in this selection.

I direct that my estate can be settled in the most expensive way possible, incurring any and all additional bonds, surety or insurance that could have been avoided had I just taken the time to prepare a will.

I agree to probate fees, legal fees and accounting fees being maximized.

I approve of bureaucrats deciding which of my children and family receive what assets.

I unconsciously disinherit any charity that I supported in life and that meant a great deal to me during my lifetime.

I direct that my assets be distributed by standard government formula without any thought at all for the proportionate needs of my survivors or my actual intentions.

I consent that the assets I worked a lifetime to acquire be squandered to pay for the arguing and settlement of the inevitable court cases that may result from this un-will.

I ask that the Courts ensure that every obscure relative of mine be entitled to a share in my estate to the detriment of the needs of the people I love and hold dear.

2
GET YOUR LIFE ON A ROLL

1. Redefine Retirement

If you were to redefine retirement as doing only those things you like to do, how would retirement look to you? It would probably include many of the things you're doing right now. It doesn't even necessarily mean that you would stop working. Lots of entrepreneurs continue to enjoy their work well into their 70s and even 80s. So as you look forward, don't feel that transitioning your business means you have to walk away from the things you enjoy doing now. Now, imagine that you retire tomorrow:

- What would you stop doing? You might default to continue doing things that you have always done or that you feel you should keep doing. However, could you drop some of them or delegate them to someone else to do without measurable consequence.

- What saps your energy? Some entrepreneurs aren't great at managing people. Dealing with performance issues, giving regular employee reviews, letting people go may all be activities that drain your energy and exhaust you. While these jobs are important and must be done by someone, does that someone have to be you? You shouldn't abdicate your responsibilities, but you might be able to delegate them.

- In a similar vein, consider activities outside your work that deplete you: the weekly bridge party that has become a chore rather than a treat; serving on a volunteer board for a cause for which you've lost your passion ... Which activities do feel you should do versus want to do that would have little or no consequence if given up?

- What would you continue to do? What parts of your life are fun and uplifting, including certain activities at work, association meetings, hobbies, time spent with family, and so on? Look for ways to enhance, expand, or incorporate more of those engagements and interactions into your daily life.

- What would you start doing? Which activities do you wish you had more time to pursue? What have you always wanted to do but still haven't gotten around to beginning? If you retired tomorrow, what activities would you really like to start doing?

2. How Do You Define Success?

Dan Sullivan, the creator of the Strategic Coach program, posed a very interesting question in one of his seminars: Is your future bigger or smaller than your past? That's a good question. It forces us to take stock of whether we've passed a point in life where we perceive that our future is diminishing in value or still getting better. It's not necessarily the number of years we have left that matters, but what we have left in the years.

Some people achieved their greatest accomplishments when they were past the normal age of retirement. Winston Churchill, Colonel Sanders, Ronald Reagan, Warren Buffett, and P.D. James are but a few who spring to mind; people who continued to be active and make significant marks well beyond the age of 65.

So while many entrepreneurs look forward to retirement with trepidation, your future could very well be bigger than your past. Consider the benefits that could be awaiting you in your new life: time, money, and wisdom.

After your transition, you may have more time to —

- exercise and maintain or regain your health,
- read,

- develop new hobbies,
- travel,
- see children or grandchildren,
- visit with siblings,
- hang out with friends,
- relax at the cottage in the north or condo in the south,
- upgrade or putter around in your home,
- volunteer and make a difference,
- go back to school and take interesting courses,
- think,
- write a book,
- start another business,
- mentor someone; or
- be a special friend to someone in need.

You'll also have more money to —

- support the hobbies or activities you want to do with the time you now have available;
- donate to a cause, institution, or family in need;
- collect art, old cars, antiques, or whatever interests you;
- invest in start-up companies or a consortium;
- establish a foundation for research, scholarships, or think tanks; or
- provide a gift to your children or grandchildren.

You'll have the wisdom to —

- share through speaking engagements;
- capture your life or perspectives in writing: a memoir, a business book, or even opinion pieces for your local newspaper; or
- coach others.

Here's another question: Would you like to be even more successful in the future than you are today?

Many entrepreneurs think this is an absurd question. They see building a successful business as the pinnacle of their life. Everything else seems boring and secondary in comparison. Selling or transitioning away from the business spells the end of success for them.

As one business owner said, "When I go to work, people show me respect. They call me Sir." They ask my opinion. They seek my approval. When I go home, what I hear is, "Take out the garbage, put your dishes in the dishwasher. No, not like that!" Hmm, where would I rather spend my time?

Have you set time aside to think about your definition of success? Have you actually put your definition on paper? As a business owner, you are more likely to have done so than most people. But have you revisited, reviewed, and updated it lately?

If you were to walk up to 100 people and ask if they would like to be successful or more successful, you would undoubtedly get a resounding yes from each and every one of them. If, on the other hand, you asked the same people to define success and what it means to them, you would probably be met with puzzled looks and fuzzy responses. In fact, most people have little or no idea what the word means to them.

Here's one possible definition:

Success is doing, being, having, and giving what you've decided to do, be, have, and give.

If you are doing what you want, being what you want, getting what you want, and giving what you want, you're successful. Otherwise, you're not. So if you want to be more successful, do more of what you want, be more of what you want, get more of what you want, and give more of what you want.

That raises the question: "What do I really, really want?"

Success is a personal choice. If you just buy into the media's concept of success, you could go crazy! To measure up to the images of success we see there, you have to drive the right car, drink the right scotch, cook with the right barbecue, luxuriate at the right spa, vacation at the right resort, and the list goes on.

This picture may be very appealing to those who are easily influenced by the desire to conform and be what others want them to be: people who are watching and competing with the neighbors. However, if you are confidently in charge of your own life, you'll see those images for what they are: just another marketing scheme that drives consumerism. Don't get me wrong. I'm not saying that the good things in life as portrayed in ads are undesirable. However, if we become shortsighted slaves to consumerism, gathering our worth from our possessions rather than from within, we set ourselves up for disillusionment and unhappiness. We all know people who have everything except personal satisfaction.

You must decide what you want rather than being unduly influenced by the values and desires of others. Ultimately, your success must be defined by you — not by your family, your peers, or your employees. They can and will give you ideas, advice, and hopefully encouragement, but the final verdict as to what is most important resides with you and you alone. After all, if you are not satisfied with your life, who is responsible? If you are happy and satisfied with your life, who is responsible? No one else can do it for you nor can anyone else shoulder the blame. Personal satisfaction is a DIY project.

If you have spent too much of your life being overly concerned about what others think or what the proper thing to do is, now is the time to open up to new possibilities. There may be something more important left to be done with your life that may or may not receive the overwhelming approval of all of your friends and family members. But remember: On our deathbeds, we don't regret what we did; we regret what we did not do.

If you don't have your own goals, you'll end up fulfilling someone else's.

3. The Value of Written Goals

I'm sure you've heard that goals should be written in order to maximize the chances of reaching them. Here are some reasons.

Written goals —

- help you become better organized;

- save you time;

- increase your effectiveness;

- provide a standard to help you measure progress;
- serve as a tool for decision-making;
- reduce conflicts between your thoughts and feelings because they clarify your expectations;
- empower your imagination;
- inspire your faith and confidence;
- channel your creativity and energy into a powerful force that is nearly impossible to defeat;
- alleviate your worry and frustration;
- improve your communications with important people in your life;
- increase your enthusiasm for life and the work you are doing;
- inspire and lead you to achievements that you previously thought impossible;
- enable you to respond maturely and effectively to negative situations;
- give purpose to your persistence and conviction;
- foster and support discipline;
- enhance your strength and endurance;
- offer you the opportunity to become self-actualized;
- plant seeds for the future; and
- create pride and enjoyment as you pursue and achieve the goals.

In his book *Always Looking Up* (Hyperion, 2009), Michael J. Fox relates the story of dealing with Parkinson's disease. For years, Fox had kept his condition from the public, but when it became harder and harder for him to hide his symptoms he announced it to the world but said he was going to continue to work. Still later, he had to admit that the daily stress and pressure of producing and acting in the weekly sitcom *Spin City* was becoming too much. One day he looked at his wife, Tracy, and said he was quitting the show. Like an entrepreneur who had worked all his life to get to this point, he realized he had to change his life and change his goals.

4. Getting Started with Goal Setting

While the concept and process of goal setting is simple, the regular discipline of actually setting and achieving goals is not.

Think about your definition of success. If you haven't decided what's really important to you in the big picture, then the goals you write down may be aimless. Or if you have an important goal that doesn't match your definition of success, then you may need to alter your definition; obviously something has changed.

4.1 Getting Your Life on a Roll (GYLOAR)

If you're successful, chances are that you are already a goal setter. You have developed a formal or informal way of looking forward, deciding what you want, and then moving in that direction.

I've been a goal setter all of my professional life. I set personal goals, sales goals, and activity goals. I have goals in binders on my bookshelf, on my computer, and in books from the myriad courses I've taken over the years. I have taken courses on goal setting, taught courses on goal setting, and created courses on goal setting.

Goal setting is obviously an important strategic process in my life. But I used to find it frustrating. I was annoyed when I didn't reach a particular goal or when I reviewed my list of goals and saw how many were left unmet. It occurred to me that part of my challenge was having too many goals and not having a way to see how they might conflict or might be tied together.

Then a few years ago, I stumbled onto an idea that has made goal setting more fun, interesting, and effective. I started out testing it on myself and since then I've tested it with many groups with enlightening results. Seasoned business owners, experienced trainers, tough-minded managers, and even entry-level employees have all found a sense of purpose and direction through this simple but effective exercise. I call the process Getting Your Life on a Roll, or GYLOAR for short.

The idea came to me at my cottage, a beautiful retreat on a secluded bay on Lake Huron. There, by myself, I looked out the open window at the clear blue water, felt the warm breeze coming off the lake, and reflected on what was really important to me. I put a roll of brown paper about 30 inches wide and 40 feet long on our dining-room table and broke out a package of Crayola markers. I took myself through a process that pulled all of my goals together. The process is not rocket science. It's a simple culmination of everything I've learned about goal setting over the past 40 years.

Using this GYLOAR process to visualize what you are moving toward will help you to get started and initiate the transition of your business.

Begin by visualizing your life at some predetermined point in the future. As Stephen Covey says, "Begin with the end in mind." (*The 7 Habits of Highly Effective People*, Simon & Schuster, 2013.) Then work backwards from there. At the end of the process, you'll have a visual connection between where you want to be and what you have to do to get there.

You can go through it on your own, or even better, consider doing it with your spouse or family. Get yourself a roll of brown kraft paper and some markers. Find a quiet spot where you can spread out the paper, ponder, dream, and plan.

4.2 Close your eyes

Start with a visualization process. You've done this quite naturally over the years as you built your business. You imagined things that would make your business better, and then you did what you had to do to make them happen. Your approach may have been a practiced and focused exercise or something you stumbled upon by accident. Sports psychologists have taught professional athletes to use visualization to stretch their physical capabilities of going faster, farther, or higher. You can use this technique, too.

Take a few deep breaths, relax, and let your mind travel to a place where you can feel at peace. It might be at your cottage, a place where you used to fish as a child, a special spot where you fell in love — only you know where that place is. Usually there is water in the picture: a lake, a river, or the ocean. Relax.

4.3 Project into the future

Imagine it's three or five years from now. Pick a date. Not just the year, but the month and day, too. Register the date in your mind. Say it over and over. Say it out loud. (But keep your eyes closed. I know. It's hard to read and keep your eyes closed at the same time.

So slowly read the following questions and idea starters out loud, record it and play it back with your eyes closed so you can better trigger your imagination.)

Today is that date. You're there right now. You have what you want, you are doing what you want, and you are the person you want to be. Everything is perfect.

What is the picture that comes to your mind? What is different about it from what you're experiencing today? What has changed? What do you see in the picture you've created? What do you hear? What do you smell? Engage your senses in the visualization process.

Think of your ideal lifestyle. Assume there are no obstacles at this point:

- You have all the time you need.
- You have all the money you need.
- You have all the skills and talents you need.
- Your relationships are positive.
- You can live anywhere you like.
- You can have anything you want.

4.4 Begin a dream list

When you were younger, you had dreams. You probably still do, but they may have diminished over the years.

Still, if you look back at what you have accomplished, you may be surprised at how much you've achieved, how many people's lives you've affected, how many ideas you've turned into reality. Unfortunately, many entrepreneurs are never happy with what they've accomplished because they are always looking at the next big thing. So let's turn that to your advantage. Let's make the next big thing the next stage of your life.

Open your roll of paper and begin to write. You are starting with the end result and working backwards. Use different colors to express your creativity. Write big or small; it doesn't matter. Draw pictures if you feel so inclined. Brainstorm. List whatever comes into your mind without judging your ability to get it. Let your imagination run wild. Create a list of all of the things that you would like to have, be, do, or give during your lifetime. Include every wish, dream, and fantasy that has ever entered your mind. Nothing is too simple or too complex.

As you think again of your ideal lifestyle, answer these questions:

- Where am I living?
- With whom am I living?
- What am I driving?
- Where do I go on vacation?
- How much money do I earn from passive income?
- What hobbies am I enjoying?
- With whom am I spending my time?
- Who are my close friends?
- What do we do together?
- What do I own that I don't own today?
- What do I no longer own that I own today?
- Who am I serving and helping with my time, money, or wisdom?
- How am I making a contribution to my community or to the world?
- How do I spend the bulk of my time?

4.5 My ideal life

If you've taken the time to answer these questions, a picture will emerge of what you want to do, be, have, and give. Now begin to describe what is included in your ideal life in more detail. At the top of your roll of paper write "My Ideal Life Includes" and think about what's really important to you. You might come up with something like the following.

My ideal life includes:
- Good health
- Financial independence
- A loving relationship
- Good friends

- Work I enjoy
- Time with my family
- Continuous learning
- Time to myself to …
- An opportunity to express my creativity
- Giving back to my community

Look like a good list? I'm afraid it's not. There are two problems with this list as far as you're concerned. First, it's my list, not yours, and second, it is too generic, too ethereal. We need to make it more tangible and specific. We also need to focus. We can't do all the things on the list at once, so let's prioritize.

First, review your list (yours, not mine) and pick the four items that you feel are the most important to you right now. Underline those four items in red. Roll out your roll a little farther. At the top of the roll, write one of your four priorities and put the word "means" after it. For example, having good health means … Then, describe in detail what good health means to you. You see, everyone has a different definition or perception of what good health means. For some people, it may mean getting in shape to run a marathon. For others, it may mean dealing better with stress or being able to go to the gym every day until they are 100 years old. For yet others, it might be becoming a nonsmoker or nondrinker. A good health list might look something like this:

Having good health means:

- I am at my ideal weight
- I do stretching exercises for 30 minutes every day
- I do aerobic exercises for at least 30 minutes, four times a week
- I eat intelligently and in moderation
- I schedule regular checkups with doctor, dentist, optician
- I sleep eight hours a night
- I have increased stamina and energy

Once you've described your first priority, go on to complete the next three and capture precisely how you would know that you were on track to get what you want.

4.6 Why do I want what I want?

Now we want to better understand why these things are important to you. What made them a priority? Roll out your paper further. Answer these questions of each goal:

- What is my motivation?

- What are the benefits that I'm looking for?

- How will reaching this goal improve my life?

Extending our example of good health might look like this:

Why do I want what I want?

- Good health
  - Without good health, nothing else matters
  - More energy for all the other things I want: hobbies, work, relationships
  - Look better and feel better
  - More productive
  - More fun

To review, you've now looked into the future and created a picture of your ideal life. That life may include work or it may not. It includes some of the people, activities, and passions already in your life and some that aren't. You have assessed what is really important to you and why.

4.7 How do I get what I want?

The next step is to assess what you have to do in order to get what you want. What obstacles do you need to get around? What's holding you back and what must you do about it? What steps or activities will get you where you want to go? If a goal is so important to you, why don't you already have it?

It's probably pretty simple. In most cases, we already know what we have to do; we just haven't done it. There's not a person in North America who doesn't know what he or she has to do to get to an ideal weight: eat less and exercise more. Knowing isn't the obstacle.

Deeper issues may be holding you back; you need to learn what they are. Why aren't you doing what you already know you should do?

What do I need to do to get what I want?

- Good health
  - Join a health club and swim three times a week
  - Bring salad for lunch
  - Park car at far end of parking lot and walk
  - Stop buying fast food
  - Start buying only nutritious food
  - Eat smaller quantities: stop feeling compelled to eat everything on my plate – push it away when I'm full
  - Exercise

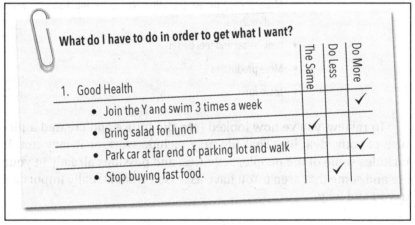

What do I have to do in order to get what I want?	The Same	Do Less	Do More
1. Good Health			
• Join the Y and swim 3 times a week			✓
• Bring salad for lunch	✓		
• Park car at far end of parking lot and walk			✓
• Stop buying fast food.		✓	

Figure 1: What Do I Have to Do?

4.8 How does my business support my lifestyle goals?

Now that you've taken time to think about what's important to you on a very personal level, take a look at how your business currently does or does not support you.

Betty owned a restaurant that served great German food. She had taken it over from her dad 20 years previously and turned a moderately successful diner into a going concern. Of course that didn't happen by accident or without a lot of dedication and hard work. Her two children now worked part time in the restaurant as they attended university. There was an unspoken expectation that they would take over the business when their mom was ready to retire.

When Betty went through the GYLOAR process, she sat back with a shocked look on her face.

"What is it?" I asked.

"It doesn't," she stated flatly.

"Pardon?"

"My current business does not support my lifestyle goals. It's all wrong! I want more time to be with my family, but the only time we spend together is when we're working and I'm telling them what to do. I want to spend more time volunteering at my church, but I work such long hours that I'm exhausted and can't get up the energy to go to the meetings. I want to improve my health, but I have no time to exercise and it's hard to lose weight when you work around food all the time."

Betty had never fully understood how much of her life she had given away to keep the family business going. She also came to the realization that it was unfair to expect her own children to follow in her footsteps. At that moment, she knew she would have to make new plans.

It's amazing how so many entrepreneurs or children of entrepreneurs are in a position today that feels more like prison than the freedom and joy that should accompany owning their own businesses.

Bill took over his father's small hydro company in Vermont. His father had taken it over from Bill's grandfather, who had started it in the late 1800s. As utilities go, it was a small company, with about 800 customers. Bill felt compelled to work the business and keep it going, more for emotional than practical reasons. He was on call 24/7. His pager was permanently glued to his hip. He did everything from invoicing and administration to climbing poles in the middle of the night to restore power. Often what were emergencies for others turned out to be minor issues in reality.

Thirty years later, he finally summoned the courage to sell the business. Once he did, he couldn't believe how good he felt. In retrospect, he wondered why he hadn't done it years earlier.

"How did you know it was really over?" I asked him.

"One day I took my pager out to the backyard and I shot it with my shotgun," he said. "I came back into the house with a mangled piece of plastic and my wife asked me what it was. I told her I shot my pager and no one was going to summon me in the middle of the night ever again."

The GYLOAR exercise will reveal whether your business and your plans over the next few years will support your ideal lifestyle. Be honest with yourself. There's no better time than the present to acknowledge whether or not you're on the right track. It might look something like this:

How does my business support my lifestyle goals?

- Provides cash flow
- Good learning opportunities
- Good team of people to work with
- Great client base to build on
- Great suppliers
- Office is close to the pool

How does my business NOT support my lifestyle goals?

- Hard to keep up with the changes; more stressful
- Hard to make time to exercise; too busy
- Hard to lose weight; too many business lunches
- Not getting enough time for myself, vacations, days off, etc.
- Not making enough money to feel I can really contribute significantly to my favorite charity
- Little time and energy left over to be an active participant with my family
- Spending too much time on the road, commuting and client meetings

4.9 Challenges

What's getting in the way? What's preventing you from getting what you want? What obstacles and roadblocks, real or imagined, are preventing you from living the life you want to live? Roll out your paper once again and write at the top, "What Challenges I Face That Could Get in the Way of My Ideal Lifestyle." Answer this question honestly. Be tough on yourself. You don't have to show this to anyone. This is for your eyes only.

What challenges do I face that could get in the way of my ideal lifestyle?

- Lack of focus and commitment
- Have to convince my spouse
- Lack of discipline
- Don't have a plan
- Lost my passion for the business
- Feel guilty about leaving my employees behind
- I'm tired and worn out; may even be depressed
- I don't know how to move forward from here; feel stuck

If you are being frank, you're revealing issues and hidden challenges that you may not have acknowledged before. You're getting in touch with what's really holding you back from doing what you currently want to do, being who you want to be, getting what you want to get, and giving what you want to give.

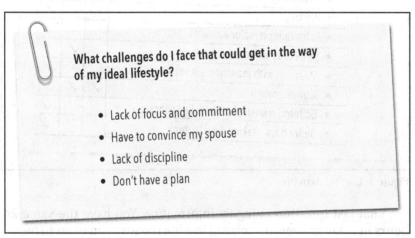

Figure 2: Challenges

4.10 What moves me toward or away from my ideal lifestyle?

Let's take it a step further. Examine your current activities and learn what you're doing every day that moves you toward or away from your ideal lifestyle. Roll out your paper once again and at the top write "Current Activities."

Current activities:

- What am I doing now that contributes to my ideal lifestyle?
- What am I doing now that detracts from my ideal lifestyle?
- What do I need to abandon in order to achieve my ideal lifestyle?

Think back over the past couple of weeks or month and imagine that you had kept a daily log of everything that you do during the day. Every activity is recorded. Where did you spend your time? What are you doing out of habit or routine? What are you doing because it's moving you forward? What are you doing that may actually be counterproductive? What do you need to abandon?

Current Activities	Abandon	Detracts	Contributes
Swimming			✓
Walking			✓
Sales calls on major accounts			✓
Sales calls on small accounts	✓	✓	
Meetings with management teams			✓
Administration	✓	✓	
Building relationships with key people			✓
Buffer days – taking time to think			✓

Figure 3: Current Activities

That last question is highly informative. You have the same 24 hours in a day as everyone else to live life the way you want to live it. You have to give up some activities in order to have time for others. You may have to give up time spent with some people in order to spend time with others whose company you prefer.

5. Business Transition Reality Check

If you've just been reading the last sections and not actually writing all your thoughts on a roll as instructed, you'd be pretty normal. That's how most people read a book. But I'm sure I've sparked some reactions, ideas, and pictures in your mind as you've been reading. Don't lose them. Pause, reflect, and write them down somewhere. Go back over these sections and make notes so that when you do get that roll of paper — and hopefully, you will — you have a starting point.

Summarize your thoughts now.

- What have you learned about yourself?

- What have you learned about your business and how it satisfies or does not satisfy your needs?

- How does it make you feel about your business in its present form? What changes do you need to make?

- What new business goals do you need to set?

- How does it impact your plans to transition your business? Will you want to do it faster? Will you want to hang on to it but in a different form?

- Will you want to change your title and responsibilities and if so, to what?

- Will you be taking more time off? How much?

- Will you be pushing for more profits and drawing more money out of the company?

- Will you be empowering your managers to take more responsibility? How?

Questions, questions, and more questions — questions that if not asked and answered will stand in the way of you and your success, no matter how you define it.

3
TRANSITION MEANS CHANGE

 Bob had everything going for him: a beautiful family, enough money, and a small but constantly growing 15-year-old business that he had built through hard work and careful planning. Then, at the age of 45, he suffered an accident that left him paralyzed and unable to manage his business independently.

At 35, Laura was the quintessential career woman, climbing the corporate ladder. However, her father suddenly developed health problems and was no longer able to muster the level of energy needed to run his business. He asked her to help; ultimately she took over his industrial supply company in New York. Within five years, she led the firm to more than double its sales and achieved her goal of providing her parents with a stable income for the rest of their lives.

Arun took a very organized approach to transition planning. When he was 55 he confirmed with his team that he would be retiring at age 60, as he had always said he would. He spent those five years increasing the value of his business. At the same time, he put the word out that he intended to sell. Six months prior to his date of retirement, he sold at a good price.

1. Change Is Constant

Change is the only constant in our lives. As we see in the previous examples, change — both positive and negative — can happen anywhere, anytime. Sometimes, as in the case of Arun, the transition is deliberate and unfolds according to the script. But often change barges in like an uninvited guest.

There are many forms of change. Change can gently creep up on you over time or violently whack you on the back of the head. You can drive change, lead change, and manage change or you can let change manage, lead, or drive you. Change can relate to a specific aspect of an individual, a business, or the economy, or it can be all-encompassing. It can arrive in a personal note like an announcement from your doctor that you need heart surgery, or in a shared reality like the economic meltdown of 2008/2009.

While it's hard to accurately foresee the outcome or impact of some changes until they actually occur, some life transitions are quite predictable. You will either grow old or you will die young. Let's hope for the former. If you get old, you will at some point become less physically and mentally capable. Whether that is the case or you do die young, here is one indisputable certainty: You will transition away from your business. It's not a question of if but when. You can do it voluntarily or involuntarily, but it will happen. And I expect you'd prefer to have the choice.

2. Complacency: The Killer of Necessary Change

Almost everyone was caught off guard by the economic storm of 2008. While there were some red flags that are easy to see with 20/20 hindsight, even the economists were still predicting growth just a few months before the maelstrom. Some people were prescient and wary enough to pull out of their stock investments near the beginning and avoid major losses. Most were not.

Imagine some of the meetings that must have taken place before the big crash in the economy.

It's June of 2008 and a meeting has been called in the boardroom. The room itself smells of money. The carpet is thick enough to sleep on. Large, ornately framed portraits of the founding fathers adorn the dark walls. The heavy oak boardroom table looks old and impressive enough to have been used by Alexander Graham Bell. Old money. Permanence. Success. It's a well-established, profitable company.

Today's meeting has been called by a nervous vice president. Conversation between the sales manager, comptroller, operations manager, and manufacturing manager is percolating around the coffee pot. After 20 minutes, the group gets down to business.

"I'm concerned about the trends I'm seeing in some of your reports," says the VP.

"We're down a bit from last year, but I'm not too worried, " the sales manager responds. "My people tell me they have a lot of orders waiting to close in the fall. You know it always slows down a bit in the summer."

"I'm not concerned at this point either," says the manufacturing manager. "I've spoken to our suppliers and they're seeing a slight dip, but I know one of them just invested half a million in new equipment and is planning to increase hiring in the next couple of months."

"I hear you," the comptroller says, looking slightly guarded. "I've heard some buzz in our association meetings, but the general feeling is cautious optimism." The operations manager joins in with, "I just hope it gets a little easier for us to hire people. As I look ahead, what I see are huge gaps in our staffing. If I could hire 20 good engineers to prepare for the future, I'd do it right now. In fact, I'm interviewing three this afternoon who look pretty good."

The VP listens but is not convinced. The evidence of a pending calamity is not yet clear but her intuition is telling her that something isn't adding up. She has a choice to make. She doesn't grasp the immediate and profound effect that her decision to push or not to push her concern forward will have on the survival and success of her business.

Similar scenarios play themselves out every day in thousands of businesses around the world. If someone raised concerns about where the economy and therefore the business was going, someone else was equally prepared to smile, pacify him or her, and negate the concern for a need to change. Complacency may well have been the biggest weakness facing businesspeople as they blindly stumbled into the toughest economy since the 1930s.

3. Boiling a Frog

For humane reasons, we haven't actually tried the following science experiment, but it is supposed to work.

- Partially fill a pot with cold water.

- Set it on a stove burner with the setting on low.

- Insert a live frog.

- Slowly increase the heat in the pot.

- Note that as the water heats up, the frog's cold-blooded nature enables it to adjust and continue to be comfortable.

- Soon, the frog becomes lethargic and lacks motivation to move unless you whack the pot and startle it into moving.

- The frog dies without even attempting escape.

Humans are also very adaptable to difficult situations. Change can sneak up on us and one day we realize we are but a degree or two from serious trouble. We all sometimes need a whack on the side of our pot.

3.1 A whack on the side of the pot

There's an old saying that goes: "If you continue to do what you've always done, you'll continue to get what you've always got." I'd like to rephrase that in light of today's reality: "If you continue to do what you've always done, your children will go barefoot and hungry."

Complacency and inertia lead to a lack of urgency. Our behavior continues as before unless something interrupts the pattern. Without a whack on the side of our pot, committees continue to hold endless meetings without outcomes or expectations. Administrators continue to work on meaningless reports. Even when we look at the facts and wonder if a change is required, our natural tendency will be to overlook clues that may be obvious to an objective outsider. In Joel Barker's research into paradigms, he learned that we see what we expect to see and will tend to deny or even be physically blind to contrary evidence. (*Paradigms: The Business of Discovering The Future*, Harper Business, 2000).

Margaret Heffernan in her book *Willful Blindness* (Anchor Canada, 2012) provides multiple examples of how seemingly normal, educated people are literally unable to perceive facts that are in conflict with their beliefs. You can see this in the polarizing stands taken by politicians and their supporters who are unable to see how their beliefs taint their perception of reality.

But if we are certain that predictable events will occur, we can prepare for them. The better prepared we are, the better equipped we are to face whatever challenges exist, many of which are in reality, also predictable.

Quick tips:

- Make time to think ahead.

- Recognize the inevitable.

- Plan for your personal transition.

- Plan for the transition of your company.

- Begin now to execute that plan even if you think you are several years away from making the change.

It's peculiar how well intentioned, intelligent, successful individuals can be caught off guard by the simple and inevitable reality of change.

Think of it as embarking on a road trip. You know how far you'll be driving. You know how far a tank of gas will take you before you have to refuel. You know that without refueling, you will run out of gas about three quarters of the way there. In fact, there is a gauge on your dashboard that tells how you're doing. At the appropriate time, you start looking for a gas station. You don't keep going, ignoring reality and hoping that you'll make it in spite of empirical proof that you won't. Yet that is what many entrepreneurs do when they briefly consider their retirement. They procrastinate, deny the inevitable, and suppress reality rather than prepare for the change that is coming.

"Never underestimate the magnitude of the forces that reinforce complacency and that help maintain the status quo." *Leading Change* (Harvard Business Review Press, 2012).

4. Why Do Most Entrepreneurs Fail to Plan for the Inevitable?

Reasons for reluctance or failure to plan vary.

You may feel that your business is stable, and you don't need to worry about impending changes such as a sale, a change in leadership, or your retirement at this point. You may be too caught up in the daily grind of running your business to set aside time for transition planning. You may simply feel that the exercise of planning for transition, a sale, or succession is too complicated and intimidating. You may want to have a transition plan in place but don't know where to begin.

A survey conducted by the Canadian Federation of Independent Businesses in 2005 captured the following responses regarding why business owners have not developed a transition or exit plan:

- 60 percent thought it's too early to plan.

- 27 percent felt they didn't have time to plan.

- 17 percent felt they couldn't find advice or tools.

- 12 percent thought it's too complex.

- 7 percent didn't want to think about leaving.

These are just excuses. Imagine that you had a senior manager in your firm that you assigned the very important task of preparing your business for transition and when you asked later how it is going, he or she tells you it's too early to plan, I don't have time to plan, I can't find advice or tools I trust, it's too complex or I don't want to think about it; how would you respond? You'd probably want to fire this person.

5. Deciding Is Not Enough

If you heeded my advice earlier in this book and have initiated the transition planning process, you can see that you have nothing to lose and everything to gain. Even if the change you plan for doesn't transpire, you will be in infinitely better shape. Why? Because transition management demands that you get to know your business even better than you do now. It requires that you hone your capabilities and nurture the competencies of your key staff. It ensures that you shape up and stay competitive and agile.

Sometimes the process of preparing your business for sale will reinvigorate your own enthusiasm and passion. Some of my clients fall in love with their businesses again once they get it running smoothly without them having to be there all the time. That's a bonus for everyone.

But planning and even deciding is not enough. Here's a riddle: There are three birds sitting on a tree. Two decide to fly south. How many birds are left? (Answer: There are three left. Two made a decision, but they haven't acted on it.)

6. The Eight Steps of the Change Process

John Kotter, again in Leading Change, suggests that there are eight steps to successfully negotiate through the change process. Consider these in the context of building a change strategy to transition your business.

1. Create a sense of urgency. As stated earlier, complacency is your enemy. When you announce that you're going to make changes, get started right away. Set short-term deadlines and actions that need to take place immediately. A sense of urgency is required to break the inertia. As the leader, you need to set the pace and the expectations. Remember: You are the one most responsible for making it happen. You are the one who will reap most of the rewards when a transition is done well, or who will face the worst consequences if it is not. If you don't set the pace, no one else will do it for you.

2. Pull together a guiding team. You're going to need people who will support you through the process and execute the actions required to make change happen. You'll need your internal management or support team and also a group of advisors who will help you set and execute the strategy for moving forward. This is too big a job to attempt to do on your own. You need experts in areas with which you are not familiar and still others to free up your time so you can focus on this major project.

3. Develop the change vision and strategy. I've said it before, but Kotter affirms the importance of knowing where you are going. Envision your personal direction and that of the company. Create your vision for what you will be doing next — what you want to do and have earned the right to do. This will help propel you toward something more appealing. Your vision for the business enables you to share the end game with your team. It enables you to work backward to determine the strategy and tactics that will get you there.

4. Communicate for understanding. Kotter suggests keeping it simple. Tell your story — often. Tell team members how the

change will unfold, how it will affect them and their positions, and how they can contribute in a positive way to the goal. Make it memorable so when the story gets repeated or relayed by others, the salient facts are all there.

5. Empower others to act. One of the challenges facing entrepreneurs who wish to prepare their businesses for sale or transition is the pressure of priorities and time. It's a rare business owner who has time left at the end of the day or week to work on the business versus in the business. But that's what you have to do. And the only way to free up your time to work on those priorities is to delegate more of your current duties. Let others make mistakes if necessary as they learn how to take on more responsibilities. Remove the barriers that prevent people from taking the actions required to get the job done. Delegate both the responsibilities, but also the authority to make decisions.

6. Produce short-term wins. Rather than trying to change the world and celebrating only when the job is done, celebrate your initial wins as soon as possible. If one of the first steps includes a leadership training program to increase the bench strength of the team, get someone to find a resource that can help you, then make the announcement that the plan is moving forward. Congratulate the people who get it done. Add more tasks only as the first ones are completed.

7. Don't let up. If you've decided to move forward and make changes, congratulations. Now you must remain single-minded in your pursuit of that change. The dogged determination that made you successful in your business needs to be re-engaged at this stage. If obstacles get in the way, fight your way around them, over them, or through them. If energy seems to be waning, pump it back up. If people lose interest, tell your story again and again until everyone understands that it is non-negotiable.

8. Create a new culture. Old habits die hard and so do traditions. You have to create new traditions, new ways of seeing the world, new approaches, and a new culture.

Now look at your plan for making the transition of your business from what it is today to what you want it to be. What steps are missing?

Abdul owned an insurance business with about 75 employees. He announced to his management team that he was going to be slowing down and selling the business in five years. There was very little reaction. Abdul was surprised. He thought that some particularly ambitious individuals would step forward and request more details. He thought that people would begin to align with this goal and start to take on more responsibility. He thought by making this announcement, things would change, but they didn't. They remained essentially the same and in some cases, where opportunities to make sound changes presented themselves, "the old way" was embraced yet again and perpetuated.

Recognizing that his team was displaying no sense of urgency, Abdul began to introduce new initiatives and goals to shake things up.

He announced that they would increase sales by 20 percent in the next year and he contracted with a sales consultant and trainer to help his skeptical team do what was necessary to make it happen. He announced that they would have a complete, highly detailed policies and procedures manual in place that would outline every duty involved to make operations run flawlessly. To help make that happen, he hired a co-op business student to manage its completion.

Abdul started taking every Friday off to work on his transition plan from his home office. He joined a Business Transition Coach Forum that met monthly. This helped him generate new ideas and support for his business transition. He took a five-week vacation – something he wouldn't have even contemplated in the past.

Still, the resistance to change was palpable. People liked Abdul and didn't want to see him retire. They had nice jobs and were comfortable with the way things were being run. They didn't like the idea of a new owner. So instead of getting on the bandwagon, some refused to co-operate with the new initiatives – not in a blatant or confrontational way but through passive-aggressive behavior. They called in sick or failed to attend sales meetings. They fed inaccurate information to the co-op student. They continued to try scheduling meetings with Abdul on Fridays or called him at home over even the most minor of issues.

It became obvious to Abdul that change was not going to happen by accident or without serious, persistent effort on his part. He knew that he himself was in for a steep learning curve about how to lead people to and through change – not just for his own sake, but for theirs.

7. Change Requires Leadership

If you don't take responsibility for the transition of your business, who the heck do you think will?

Like Abdul, you may have announced your intentions to slow down or prepare your business for sale. But have you pushed it? Have you actively initiated specific changes that put your intentions into play? Or have you sabotaged the plan yourself, saying one thing but doing another? Have your actions and behaviors aligned with the words you are using to communicate or does your body language still say "status quo?"

Some changes you can predict and control, and some you can't. You need to decide what changes you want to make, and then make them. Decide which changes are inevitable and plan for the best way to make them work for you. Maintaining the status quo and hoping things will work out for the best is no way to get what you want. Worksheet 2 (available on the downloadable forms kit; see the back of the book for instructions for accessing it) should get you started considering all of the changes that await you.

4
CHOOSE YOUR BEST OPTION FOR TRANSITION

In this chapter I provide an overview of typical transitions available to business owners so you can weigh which one best suits you and your unique situation. Within each of these options are subsets to choose from. Whichever route you choose, you should definitely speak with your advisors to fine tune your decision.

Looking at things from a broad perspective, here are your options when it comes to business transitions.

1. Make time to plan and prepare the business for sale. Then sell it, ideally at the time of your choosing to the buyer of your choosing for your preferred price. Buyers may include family members, employees, competitors, suppliers, or investment bankers. A subset of this option is to merge your company with someone else's.

2. Work until you die or become disabled and leave the problem of what to do with your business to your family or managers.

3. Work hard until you burn out or get fed up and then sell to the first buyer you meet, probably not for your preferred price.

4. Wind the business down and close it.

5. Keep the business, but develop people to run it for you so you can do what you want and continue to receive a personal income from the business. Then, when the inevitable happens, you have communicated a plan for the orderly transfer of the business in a predetermined process that minimizes the negative impact on your survivors.

Since you're reading this book, we'll assume that your preferred choices would be 1 or 5, but remember, option 2 can happen any time, without your consent. For that reason, we'll focus on these three options and touch lightly on the other two.

1. Option 1: Preparing to Sell

Mario and I were sitting in a small cafe in El Paso, Texas, discussing the sale of his business. His company, a supplier to the aerospace industry, was generating about $75 million in sales the year before he sold it. It was highly profitable and over the previous five years had doubled its sales.

I asked him why he sold his business.

"It was a business decision like many others I'd made," he said. "Selling was a logical step in the evolution of the business and myself. I was getting older. My sister would have taken it over if anything happened to me and frankly I didn't believe she was capable. Also, I needed to do some restructuring to offset the punitive tax structure."

"How long did it take you between the time you decided to sell and the completion of the deal?"

"Seven years. I started planning it in my head in the year 2000. Then I got really focused six years later and thought I could finish it in 6 months, but it still took 18 months."

Mario's experience underlines an important lesson I heard from many of the former business owners I interviewed: Selling your business is a process, not an event. It takes time. Mario estimates that he invested well over two thousand hours in the process of selling his business, over and above his regular CEO duties, during that critical period.

Brian was a very successful real estate developer in Houston. He grew his business to the point where it was building and selling more than 700 single-family housing units annually.

He sold his business shortly before the housing crisis hit the USA in 2007/2008.

If he had waited two or three years, it would have cost him millions. He chose the timing of the sale and fortunately for him, he chose well.

"I knew the bubble would burst at some point," he said.

1.1 Preparing your business for sale

There are fundamental questions you have to answer before you plan to sell your business. Do you in fact have something to sell? Is it a business that someone else would be willing to buy? Is your own contribution and presence in the business so critical that it would flounder without you? Could it even exist without you? Could someone else (who isn't your clone or identical twin) run the business and make it profitable?

If you have to honestly admit that in its present condition your business would fail without you, you have a lot of work to do to get it ready to sell. We'll deal with this in more detail in Chapter 7, but you should begin today to build your business so that at the very least it is worth more than the depreciated value of your furniture and equipment.

1.2 Timing is critical

If you are looking ahead, planning to sell, how do you know the best time to exit? Should you sell when the market is on the upswing? When your company is operating at peak performance? Or should you simply wait until you are ready to call it quits?

The reality is that the best possible offer for your business can crop up at the most inopportune time.

Timing is one of the critical factors that determine the success of a sale. The best time to sell may be simply when someone is really keen to buy. Many business owners have described having a great offer come out of the blue, when they were least expecting it. Those who were prepared were able to command a better price.

Take the case of Mickey MacDonald. His Halifax-based company had 44 percent of the cell phone market in Atlantic Canada when Alliant approached him with an offer to buy it. Macdonald had succeeded to the point where he was no longer flying under the radar of the bigger players and they wanted his market share. He had a choice: sell to a large multinational, or enter into an all-out war with them.

Macdonald sold. When I asked him if he had been ready to sell, he replied that even though he hadn't wanted to sell yet, in effect he was always preparing his business for sale. He was always increasing sales, training his people, building the brand, winning customers on exceptional service, and running a tight ship.

In other words, MacDonald had a proactive performance and transition plan in place, enabling him to get a good price for his business, preserve the jobs of employees, and free himself up to try his entrepreneurial talents in three new businesses.

1.3 The biggest sale of your life

The sale of your business will be one of the most important events in your life. Unlike most other business decisions, this is one that you might make only once. While there is no way you can predict the exact time of your sale or the price your business will be able to command, there are a few things you can do to increase the odds in your favor.

Sometimes you do have to sell your business more than once. Scott in Florida sold his insurance company to a consortium that also bought nine other insurance firms. He kept control of the business until the last dollar was paid, but after two years the overall group was not doing as well as expected and the company defaulted on its payments. Scott took back the company and sold it again for even more than he got the first time.

If you were selling your house, what would you do to ensure that it gets the best price? You might start with the superficial: giving the walls a fresh coat of paint, changing the curtains, and replacing the leaky faucet. But buyers will look deeper. They'll dig in to the less obvious, structural issues such as the age and energy efficiency of the windows, the cracks in the foundation, the rot in the floor joists.

The same principle applies to your business: The more solid it is, through and through, the better your chances are of getting paid what you want for it. And no, it is not just about the price. You've probably devoted much of your life to building and nurturing your baby, so you want to ensure that it isn't ugly. There's a sense of pride and dignity in selling a business that's in excellent shape.

In order to sell your business well at the right time, you need to be ready to sell at any time. The first and often the most difficult step is deciding that you want to get started. In his book *Every Family's Business* (Detente Financial Press, 2009), Thomas Deans argues that your business should always be for sale and you shouldn't make any secret of it.

The goal you want to attain by the time you retire plays a crucial role in deciding your business strategy and operations. Most entrepreneurs who do realize the significance of transition planning and preparing for retirement focus almost exclusively on the financial aspects. They look at ways to maximize the net worth of their business. They try to balance the need for profitability with the desire to set aside some personal savings for their post-retirement life. In the process, they may fail to consider other fundamental aspects of transition planning, including the most basic one: what they want to do with their business when they retire.

1.4 Your possible buyers

1.4a Selling to your family

If you own a family business, chances are you want to keep it in the family.

A strong emotional component seems to trump logic when it comes to family businesses, and only you know whether passing the business on to family is the right decision. A survey conducted by PWC indicated that almost half of family business owners plan to pass the business on to the next generation. That said, "47% of them don't actually have a succession plan in place and 27% have not involved the next generation in preparing for these changes." ("Retirement pushes Canadian private company owners to keep, sell or transfer their business," PWC.com, accessed March, 2020.)

There are many questions that you will want to consider if you are thinking of selling to family members. Again, I would recommend *Every Family's Business* as a good primer. In it, Thomas Deans takes a contrarian view of family business succession. He advocates that it is more important to maintain and enhance the family wealth as opposed to the family business because they may be mutually exclusive. If the family business is the best way to continue to build family wealth, that's great. But there may come a time when it is in the family's best interest to sell the business, take the money, and invest it elsewhere.

Suppose that Junior is interested in the business only because you expect him to take it over and he wants to please you. Suppose that you expect Junior to buy shares but Junior expects you to give them to him, but you've never actually had that discussion. Imagine that given a choice between running your manufacturing business or starting her own, your daughter would rather start a marketing company. Which is more likely to succeed in the long run? Which will make her happier? Would you rather saddle your kids with a business that they feel obligated to maintain, or give them the freedom to succeed with their own dreams?

Deans also asserts that the worst thing you can do for both the business and your children is to gift shares to your children. He contends that it's better to give them money and offer the shares for sale, letting them decide if they want to use the money to buy shares in your company or for something else. Their decision about how to use the money is a powerful message.

Deans suggests that every year a business owner and his or her family (if the family is involved) sit down and answer what he calls the "The 12 Questions," one of which assesses a conscious decision to sell or not to sell in the next year. Here are six of the questions:

1. (Both parent and child must answer if each holds stock.) Are you interested in selling your stock? If yes, to whom?

   This question opens the dialogue and helps to uncover the motivation of the seller. If the answer is yes, then why? If no, why not?

2. (To be answered by the child.) Are you interested in buying stock and acquiring control?

   It may have been implied or assumed that this was the intention, but you may have never actually had this open discussion. What if the parent wants to sell but the child doesn't want to buy? What if the child wants to buy, but the parent doesn't want to sell? What if the parent wants to sell but keep control? This question flushes a lot of possibilities into the open.

3. (To be answered by both parent and child.) Do you understand and agree, in the interest of maximizing shareholder value, that this business can be sold to a third party at any time? Yes or no?

This question acknowledges that the business is always for sale and that it could be sold to a third party. If Junior is interested in being the owner, he needs to speak up. It also raises the question of compensation for the child. If he thinks he is busting his butt at minimum wage for a future carrot that may never materialize, he has every right to open up the compensation discussion and make sure he is being paid what he is worth. This leads to the next question.

4. (To be answered by the parent.) I agree that within the next 60 days I will put in place a special compensation formula for my child in the event that the business is sold in the next five years. Yes or no?

Selling the business to a third party may require your daughter to continue on contract for a period of time as part of the deal. What does she get for her loyalty and hard work if not the company shares? Better to have that discussion in advance than after the fact when expectations on both sides could be as far apart as the sides of the Grand Canyon.

5. (To be answered by both parent and child.) As a fundamental principle I understand that from time to time we will receive unsolicited offers from third parties to acquire the business. These offers will be considered and accepted at the discretion of the controlling shareholder and supported by the child. Yes or no?

The business is better positioned to succeed if both parent and child agree on this question and have also decided on special compensation for family members in the event of the sale. That said, this question could uncover a lot of "what ifs" for discussion.

6. (To be answered by the parent.) In preparation for the annual update of this blueprint I will arrange for an updated valuation of the business and will calculate whether there is an appropriate amount of insurance in place. I will furnish evidence that this has been done and that the estate taxes will not impair the ability of this corporation to function after my death. Yes or no?

You can see that the questions are very direct and you can't fudge the answers. There's no room for "maybe" or "sort of" or "when I have more time." It's yes or no. If parent and child really care about their relationship and family wealth as opposed to merely keeping the business in the family, the questions force some very honest communications. Deans suggests having an annual formal meeting in which the family addresses and revisits his questions. You might want to hire a facilitator to lead the discussion and keep it on track, at least for the first meeting.

1.4b Selling outside the family

If selling to family is not your preference, there are other options.

Employees: Selling to your employees is a good option if you have time to execute it and have confidence in your people. You are likely to end up holding a loan or mortgage that is repayable over time because the employees probably are not in a position to buy you out with cash.

1. You may have a senior manager, or right-hand person who you feel has what it takes to run the business.

2. You may have a small group of senior managers who would like to purchase shares and keep the business going.

3. You may implement an employee share ownership plan (ESOP), inviting many employees to be part of the ownership group. An ESOP may enable you to prepare your business for sale so you can exit with the money you need for retirement while creating a lasting corporate legacy.

One of Canada's leading authorities on ESOPs, Perry Phillips, has written two books on the subject. At a recent seminar, he shared some interesting statistics about how ESOPs are helping business owners and companies change and thrive, even in difficult markets. Quoting a study by the Toronto Stock Exchange comparing ESOP and non- ESOP public companies, in his book *Employee Share Ownership Plans* (Wiley, 2001) he stated that ESOP companies had a —

- 123 percent higher five-year profit growth,

- 95 percent higher net profit margin,

- 24 percent greater productivity,

- 2 to 10 percent premium on the stock market,

- 92.26 percent return on average total equity,

- 65.52 percent higher return on capital, and

- 31.54 percent lower debt/equity ratio.

ESOPs are not as common in Canada as they are in the United States where tax treatments are more favorable. Still, Phillips believes and has shown that with or without government assistance, the benefits of setting up an ESOP far outweigh the disadvantages, if a company has the right environment and motivation to make it work. With statistics like these, it's worth considering this option for transitioning a business.

Why do ESOPs work? According to Phillips, they help address many of the workplace issues that plague employers today: productivity, competitiveness, survival, succession, recruiting, and retention.

It's logical that when employees have tangible ownership of the company they work for, they are more inclined to do what is necessary to drive it to peak productivity and profitability. Think about how hard business owners work. While employee shareholders will rarely have as much drive and passion as the founder, partial ownership helps them narrow the gap and become more conscious of cutting expenses, reducing waste, and encouraging coworkers to be more efficient. They will be more inclined to speak out when they see someone goofing off or stealing. They will take a more active interest in the fiscal health and well-being of "their" business. They will keep their eyes open for others who would be positive additions to the organization, so recruitment challenges and costs are reduced. They will be less inclined to leave because of petty differences or small gaps in pay.

"But," warns Phillips, "the mere fact of setting up an ESOP does not automatically transform a corporate culture. It takes more than a shareholder's agreement; employers and employees must embrace the special dynamics of share ownership and commitment."

Success requires a 100 percent buy-in from the current owner and genuine participation by the employees. Studies in the US show that ESOP companies with a participation component outperform those without. "Participation means that the employees take on the responsibility of their particular job as well as the accountability that goes along with it by participating in decision-making in their sphere of influence within the organization," wrote Phillips.

A successful transition to an ESOP doesn't happen overnight or by chance. It requires a thoughtful, detailed approach. It requires commitment and participation from the owner and employees. Philosophy and values must be aligned in a culture of transparency and trust. Phillips adds that "the goal of most ESOPs is to have each employee reach his or her maximum potential as a person and as an employee." He suggests that all employees get training to be the best that they can be in their areas of responsibility.

In my opinion, Phillips's work and success with ESOPs both reinforces and aligns with the holistic and positive approach that I favor. A company that taps into the strengths and abilities of its employees: encourages full ownership and participation; has a leader who is willing to be transparent and share control; and develops and trains people to become as good as they can be is growing its business intelligently. A carefully planned and executed ESOP combined with a robust people-development program can help you transition your business and leave a strong legacy.

After his partner's unexpected death, Dino Ditta of Orange County, California, had to buy out his estate. Neither he nor his partner had planned for that.

The trauma generated from that experience spurred Ditta to put a five-year plan in place to build the business and prepare it for sale. He wasn't that old, but he had the attitude that an entrepreneur should have: He looked at his business as an entity that was built to sell.

Ditta didn't get his full five years in before he received an offer. It wasn't as high as he wanted or what he would have expected if he had been able to go another year, but it was good enough that with some negotiating, he was able to accept the deal.

Competitors: Your competitors may be interested in purchasing your business because they want your market share, client base, employees, intellectual property, location, revenues, or all of the above — they might even want your losses for tax advantages.

Competitors may pay a premium for your business because they see it as a strategic purchase that leverages their own business. The combined business may give them volume to negotiate discounts with suppliers. It may enable efficiencies in shipping or doubling the number of accounts a salesperson can handle in his or her territory.

Competitors may just be happy to get you out of the market. If your goal is to maximize the value of your sale and get most of it in cash, then selling to a competitor is definitely a viable option.

Suppliers: Your major supplier may be interested in purchasing your business in order to maintain control of its product placement in the market.

Partners: You may already have a partner who owns shares in your business. If that partner is interested in carrying on the business, he or she is a natural for buying the balance of your shares. If you don't have a partner, you might consider looking for one. I took on a partner for 50 percent of one of my businesses and he purchased the balance five years later. It was a win-win agreement.

Investors: Many individuals, consortiums, and funds are looking for places to invest their money for a healthy return on that investment. If your company is consistently profitable, in a good market with a solid management team, a good client base, and a good story to tell, you may find investors who are interested in buying your business.

2. Option 2: Work Hard until You Die or Become Disabled

While some amount of uncertainty and even trauma accompanies every kind of transition, sudden changes can be devastating to the business, especially if they are tragic. The sudden death or incapacity of a business owner or leader is among the most common causes of business failures. But how do you prepare your business for life after your death?

We don't like to think of dying or being disabled, especially when we are still in the prime of our lives. We like to believe that we will lead a healthy, active life until we're 104. Then we expect to die painlessly and peacefully in our sleep, leaving everything perfectly planned out for our business and for our family (including our great-grandchildren). I love that fantasy. While premature death or disability doesn't happen to everyone, the responsible thing to do to protect your family, your business, and your employees is to insure against such possibilities. It is important to put a plan in place now to take effect when the unexpected happens.

Tragic events differ from the other transitions in part because of their sudden nature. But they also carry the additional element of increased shock for all of those involved. In the case of Bob, introduced in the last chapter, his accident shook his family and business to their very core.

 Bob was a responsible family man and confident entrepreneur. Though he was close to and open with many of his trusted employees, he didn't think it necessary to discuss the finer strategic aspects of business with them. Not one to mix family with business, he didn't consider it important to discuss his future plans with his wife, either.

After the accident, he was unable to talk. During this period, his wife, Mary, who was determined not to let the growing company crash, managed to carry on business the best she could with the help of the management team. But there were several times when they were stuck wondering which direction to take and whether Bob would have approved of their decision. Bob had a wealth of knowledge and experience, and a large network; advantages that were not written down anywhere; advantages that he had never shared with anyone.

These were difficult times. The strain of supporting a struggling business as well as an ailing husband took its toll on Mary and their family.

2.1 A business continuity plan

Having a business continuity plan in place makes it easier for your family, partners, or employees to cope with a tragic event. It also frees them of the burden of having to step in unwillingly and take charge. Preparation can reduce or eliminate ugly conflicts or confrontations about ownership, leadership, or the sale of the business.

If you haven't done so already, speak with your lawyer and prepare a will. Some lawyers suggest that business owners have two wills. Have a discussion with key stakeholders, stating who will take charge in case of your death and how the assets and liabilities of the business will be transferred. You should also appoint a power of attorney in case you become incapacitated. If you have a partnership or shareholder's agreement, your written agreement should state the course of action to be taken in case one of the partners dies or is unable to continue in the business.

As you think through these issues, you may come to the conclusion that you're facing some serious problems, ones to which you don't have all the answers. For example, without proper insurance coverage, the taxes triggered on death could bankrupt a business. A long-term disability foisted upon you as the owner could handicap the business as well. In the absence of a will and clear instructions, the government could decide what happens to your business.

Be sure to discuss these issues with your family as well as a capable financial and insurance advisor, preferably one with a Chartered Financial Planner (CFP) and Chartered Life Underwriter (CLU) designation. A sharp advisor will help you to deal with these issues in a way that represents your best economic interests and preferences.

2.2 Dying with your boots on

The movie poster of the old film *They Died with Their Boots On*, starring Errol Flynn and Olivia DeHavilland, shows Flynn in an American Civil War uniform with sword raised in defiance while the beautiful young DeHavilland looks on fearfully, clearly wondering what will happen to her when he is gone. Heroism aside, I wonder if those who died with their boots on made provisions for their loved ones in the case of their deaths.

"I can't see myself retiring." "My work is my life." "I plan to keep working until I die." "I want to go out with my boots on."

I've heard variations on this sentiment from many of the entrepreneurs I've worked with over the decades and yes, I will confess to uttering some of them myself. The thought of retiring is somewhat frightening and for those who do really enjoy their work, there doesn't seem to be any good reason to retire. Then again, many people who in their 50s said they were never going to retire changed their mind by the time they hit their 60s. As with most things, it's wise to keep your options open.

The good thing about being a business owner is that the choice is almost entirely in your hands. You don't need to retire until you feel you are ready for it. However, choice also implies responsibility. While the choice is yours, so is the burden of zeroing in on the right time for your exit and of making sure you have at least provided for those who eventually will be affected by it.

3. Option 3: Burn out and Sell to the First Buyer

Alas, I have some personal experience with this one. Several years ago, I was working like a typical entrepreneur, putting in ridiculous hours and running myself ragged. I was running three businesses at the time. One of them was not going the way I wanted. It seemed to me that the easy way out of the pain it was causing was to put it up for sale.

I had one prospective buyer, a manager in the firm who had been surreptitiously creating many of the headaches I was experiencing. I didn't fully understand that at the time, so I was blindsided by his insulting offer to purchase the business at 15 percent of my estimate of its worth. When I realized that he had been deliberately manipulating numbers and had created a serious cash-flow crunch to jeopardize my personal finances, I escorted him and his co-conspirators to the door. The ringleader was surprised. He thought he had backed me into a corner with no resources left to resist his hostile takeover.

This experience reinforced for me the importance of learning what to do, and what not to do, in preparing to sell a business. Here are some hard-learned don'ts:

- Don't sell when you have only one prospective buyer. Unless he or she is really anxious to purchase, you are negotiating from a position of weakness. The more bidders you have, the better the auction.

- Don't assume that with little effort on your part, someone will someday show up at your door and make you a reasonable offer to purchase your business. It's probably not going to happen.

- Don't wait until you are burned out, exhausted, and fed up to start planning for the sale of your business. Prospective purchasers will smell your desperation and take advantage of you in negotiations.

- Don't assume that the buyer is your friend. He or she is looking for the best deal possible and his or her gain is your loss.

- Don't negotiate the deal on your own. You're too emotionally involved to be objective.

4. Option 4: Wind down the Business and Close It

During the 2008 economic meltdown, bankruptcies soared. Many business owners just gave up. What a sad way to end a dream.

You may own a small business built on the strength of your personality, made up of only a handful of people. If so, you are at risk of simply closing and leaving them in the lurch when you are ready to quit. There is a thin line between being self-employed and running a business. If the business's real strength and value revolves around you as the owner and couldn't survive without you, then it is probably not a business that can be sold — at least not for much money. You might get some residual value by selling your customer list to a competitor, or selling your office furniture and equipment for cents on the dollar.

Like the work involved in having a garage sale, closing a business can be distressing, disheartening, and time-consuming compared to the financial gain received.

Barry was nearly 70. He was a successful business owner who had grown his industrial equipment distribution business to a point where it was earning him a good living. He was hoping to pass the business on to his son, Jeff.

Jeff, a married man with two children, was working with his dad on sales, but his heart wasn't in it. He wanted to make the business successful because it would be his father's primary source of retirement income. But he wasn't in love with the business and was only moderately successful in sales.

After listening to each one's perspectives, I helped them to realize that transferring the business to Jeff would be disastrous for both of them. Jeff would be saddled with running a business he didn't like and would continue to feel guilty about not meeting his father's expectations. Barry, a consummate salesperson, would always be worried that his income and, more importantly, his reputation were at risk. He would be constantly frustrated by Jeff's lack of ambition and sales.

We set Jeff free to pursue his own dream and Barry wound down the business and sold his client list to a competitor. If Barry had started five years earlier to groom a successor who was as passionate as he was, he might have had more to sell.

If you want to leverage your past efforts into future financial return, the better approach is to start now to build a business versus a practice. (We define a business as something that will run and continue to earn revenue and profits even while you are on vacation.)

In his book *Cashflow Quadrant* (Warner Books, 1999) Robert Kyosaki explains that there are only four ways to make money: employment, self-employment, owning a business, and from investments. He places them in a chart like in Table 2.

A couple specific comments really hit home to me. First, he said that people who are only on the left side of the chart will never become financially wealthy because there are limitations to how much they earn and if they stop working, the income dries up. Only owning a business or having investments allows you the opportunity to continue to make money even when you are sleeping, on vacation, or during a disability. The second point was that the more successful you are as an employee or self-employed, the harder you have to work. So true! As you succeed, you are in more demand. But the more successful you are as a business owner or investor, the less you have to work. You have more options.

Table 2
Cashflow Quadrant

Number of Employees	Percentage of All Businesses	Number That Sells
< 10	80%	1 in 5.5
10-20	9%	1 in 4
21-100	8%	1 in 3.5
> 100	3%	1 in 3

5. Option 5: Keep the Business

You might want to hang on to the business as an investment. If it is running well, it might make sense to continue to draw an income from it while deliberately pulling back, slowing down, or removing yourself from day-to-day operations.

This is the amazing opportunity you have created for yourself as an entrepreneur! If you have prepared well, you have the option, the choice, and the freedom to decide how and when to take your leave. You can sell or not sell.

Keeping the business doesn't mean keeping the status quo. Your bank, suppliers, and employees will still wonder what is going to happen, because let's face it: None of us is getting younger. I'm sure even Bob Cratchit must have wondered what would happen to him and his family when Scrooge died. A business in an indefinite holding pattern is a business running out of gas. You're either continuing with a forward thrust or you are stalling and will sputter. We'll spend more time on this in future chapters, but here's a sneak peek.

1. Take stock of where you are now and where you would like to be in the future, and assess the gap.

2. Form your advisory group.

3. Create a strategic growth plan in writing: something you can visualize, get excited about, and communicate to others.

4. Work on the business, not in the business. This concept is well documented in Michael E. Gerber's book, *The E-Myth Revisited* (Harper Business, 2004).

5. Put the right people in the right roles doing the right things to advance your strategic growth plan.

6. Work to your strengths and the strengths of your team. If you have done a good job of selecting the right people to work with you — that is, their strengths coincide with the activities that will produce the results you need in your business — then let them do what they do best.

7. Develop and train your people so you increase their capabilities, build teamwork, enhance their loyalty, and make them more valuable as one of the assets you can sell as part of your business.

8. Delegate, delegate, delegate! You can't sell the business if you're doing all the interesting, complicated, and fun projects yourself. Let people learn by doing and making mistakes, then provide them with coaching to help them succeed.

9. Take more vacations and see how people manage when you're not there. Provide feedback and coach as required.

10. Get your ego out of the way. Celebrate when your people do as good as or a better job than you might have done.

With these ten points as a guide, you can enhance your options and have even more freedom to choose.

There is a map of your options and possible paths to follow, in Figure 4.

Raymond, a financial advisor, tells an interesting story about wishful thinking: He had a conversation with a client who was thinking of selling his business and asked him what he thought it was worth.

"Fourteen million dollars, " he replied.

That seemed like a rather inflated number, so he probed a little further and asked him how he came to that number.

"Well, I have a number of loyal employees that I want to reward with some cash, I want to give a million to each of my three kids, and I need about $7 million to retire."

In other words, he thought the business was worth what he wanted it to be worth, not necessarily what someone would actually pay for it! Oddly enough, I think a lot of entrepreneurs value their business that way.

Worksheet 3 (available on the downloadable forms kit; see the back of the book for instructions for accessing it) should get you thinking about the tasks involved with selling a business.

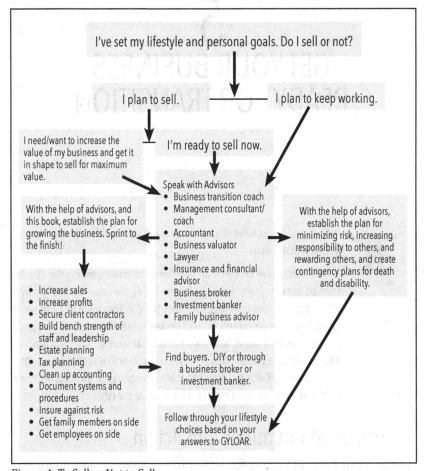

Figure 4: To Sell or Not to Sell

5
GET YOUR BUSINESS
READY FOR TRANSITION

"What would you have done differently if you could sell your business again?" I asked Mark.

"I would have broken it up into three companies, selling the one and keeping the other two," he said. "For the buyer, the value was really only in one of the business divisions. The other two divisions were just add-ons as far as they were concerned. If I had backed those divisions out a couple of years earlier, they would have paid the same amount for the main business and I could have had another $5 million in assets that I could have kept or sold separately. Because I didn't do that early enough in the negotiations or before we even started, I left a lot of money on the table."

1. Turn Good Intentions into Action

Getting your business ready for transition or sale is a culmination of all of the improvements you have planned over the years but have not (yet) implemented. It's like replacing windows, carpeting in the living room, fixing the leak in the basement, and putting in a new kitchen once you've decided to sell the house. All of your good intentions to make your business more successful need to be completed now in preparation for creating maximum wealth. Yes, it's time to accelerate.

This is the sprint to the finish. If you want to make the transition in five years, you have only five years left to make it happen. And you know from experience how quickly five years can fly by.

2. Take Stock: Where Are You Now?

We've done some of the work of taking stock in an earlier chapter. I asked you to look into the future, visualizing where you would like to be as an individual and how you would like your personal lifestyle to unfold. Now it's time to look at how your business can provide the wealth or resources necessary to bring that to fruition.

Earlier I shared the story of the business owner who thought his business was worth $14 million — not because that was its true worth but because that's what he needed to execute his personal goals. Arriving at a number is a good start, but it must be realistic so you have the foundation from which to begin.

3. How to Estimate the Value of Your Business

Every industry is different, and there are a variety of ways in which businesses are valued. If you understand how prospective buyers look at acquisitions and value those purchases, you can do a better job of maximizing the value of your business as you plan to sell it. As noted in the story earlier, you might also be able to remove assets from the business without affecting the final price.

Getting the right appraisal of the value of your business is difficult at the best of times. So many factors can affect the value of your business; a number placed on it today could be completely off base within months. Let's look at some of the considerations.

3.1 Will a strategic buyer or a financial buyer purchase your business?

A strategic buyer may pay a much higher price than its actual appraised value if it means —

- removing you as a competitor;

- obtaining your client list, which will dovetail nicely with the buyer's strategic plan for expansion;

- taking over your experienced and successful sales force;

- gaining new technology or complementary intellectual property;

- acquiring a solid management team that knows how to run a business;

- penetrating a new market that would cost significant dollars to open on his or her own; or

- fulfilling the mandate of growth dictated by his or her shareholders.

3.2 Will it be an asset or stock purchase?

Purchasing assets is usually more favorable to the buyer because he or she can choose to include or exclude certain assets from the offer, and it means not accepting historic environmental or legal liabilities. It is usually less favorable to the seller because of the different methods of taxation. An asset sale is not ideal if you really want to wash your hands of the business and all responsibility because it could leave you liable for past sins, even years after the sale is completed.

3.3 Rule of thumb formulas are often used in valuing businesses

You should be wary of rule of thumb formulas, because each business is unique. That said, certain industries evolve in predictable enough trajectories to value them a certain way. For example, Frederick Lipman in *The Complete Guide to Valuing and Selling Your Business* (Prima Lifestyles, 2001) delineates these industry multipliers:

- Insurance agencies tend to sell at one to two times annual gross commissions.

- Real estate agencies tend to sell at two to three times annual gross commissions.

- Restaurants tend to sell at three to five times annual gross sales.

These rules can still be off the mark, depending on the profitability, location, and infrastructure of the specific business for sale. The owner of an insurance agency in Florida told me he sold his business for seven times earnings, which was unheard of in his industry. The reason: He had systematized his business so well that it could be managed successfully by relatively low-paid employees. They could simply execute the extremely well-defined policies and procedures he had put in place. "I had binders and systems for everything," he said. "The buyer was so impressed with how well things ran without me being there, he convinced himself he could run the business from a distance while the staff continued to do their jobs."

3.4 Many businesses are valued on accounting earnings or income

This is calculated by taking your earnings before interest, taxes, depreciation, and amortization (EBITDA) and multiplying that number by a relevant multiplier.

3.5 Other ways to estimate the value of businesses

Other ways to estimate value include discounted cashflow methods; comparable company methods; comparable transaction methods; asset-accumulation methods; the value of goodwill and intangibles; the value of discretionary cash-flow; and the value if assets were liquidated.

Whole books have been written dealing solely with this topic; I suggest that you peruse some of them (see the Resources on the downloadable kit that came with this book) or simply speak to your accountant or business broker to determine the best method of valuation for your industry in general and your business in particular. Knowing in advance how your business is valued from the perspective of a buyer is the most important thing at this stage. When you know what buyers are seeking, you can accentuate your strengths, minimize your weaknesses, eliminate any deal-killers, and enhance the true value of the business from their perspective, not yours.

3.6 Speak to an expert

Valuing a business is a professional skill and your business is unique. There are several ways to value a business and the way that's in your best interest depends upon many factors. You can find business valuators in North America at the following websites:

- The American Society of Appraisers: www.appraisers.org

- National Association of Certified Valuators and Analysts: www.nacva.com

- CVB Institute (Canadian Chartered Business Valuators) cbvinstitute.com

- Institute of Business Appraisers: www.nacva.com/go-iba

4. Factors Affecting the Valuation of Your Business

Regardless of the method of valuation, certain factors will either increase or decrease the value of your business, such as:

1. The quality and quantity of your customer relationships, how long you've retained them, and what percentage any one customer makes up of your total sales. Too much reliance on any one customer or industry could be perceived negatively.

2. The proprietary products, patents, intellectual capital, processes, or services of the business.

3. The strength, capabilities, and versatility of your management team and the commitment they have to staying with the company. Do you have contracts with key managers? Have you considered offering bonuses to entice them to stay until a certain date? Could you offer bonuses based on the final price you get for the business so they have an incentive for helping you maximize the sale value?

4. The quality of employee relationships and the commitment they have to the company. Is the company unionized? Are the contracts up to date? Have there been any bitter disputes? Also, how would you rank as an employer of choice? Do people want to work for you? Do you have a bulging file of employment applications?

5. The consistency and trending of revenues and profits. Up is good. Down is bad. Do you have a predictable cash flow? Do you know how to manage it?

6. The age, quality, and state of repair of your equipment and buildings.

7. Net book value: the total assets versus liabilities on your financial statements.

8. The organization, timeliness, and accuracy of your accounting systems.

9. The impact of your personal income and benefits on the bottom line. If you have been taking more from the company than you would have to pay a president hired to replace you, recast your statements in order to normalize that impact.

10. The clearly defined and followed policies, procedures, and systems that make your business run smoothly.

11. Don't underestimate the value of a great story that explains where your business is headed. Buyers are more interested in the future value of the company than its historical value. That's what they are buying: the ability of your business to create future profits and value for them and their shareholders.

5. How to Define Your Transition Goal

If you did the exercises suggested in Chapter 2, you have a picture of what you want your personal future to look like. You've laid it out and you know where you're heading. A little work with a financial advisor will help you translate that vision into a number and what's required to make that work. Let's work through an example based on the assumption that your number is $3 million after taxes. This amount will enable you to —

- provide some rewards and incentives for loyal employees who have increased the value of your business;

- give a gift to your children who did grunt work for you as they earned their university tuition;

- bestow a donation upon your favorite charity;

- eliminate all outstanding personal debt; and

- take a $75,000-per-year income for the rest of your life, based on a modest interest rate.

Let's assume further that you determine, after speaking to a business valuator, that your business is only going to provide $2 million in the current state of the economy. This may or may not be a problem, depending on your timing. I would venture to say that if you plan to sell in the next 12 months, you do have a problem. But if you're planning ahead and have time on your side, it's no problem at all. In fact, what you have now is a new, clearly defined goal you can sink your teeth into.

If you follow the advice of the goal-setting gurus, you'll know that you should have a SMART goal — one that is:

- Specific

- Measurable

- Achievable

- Realistic

- Timely

I like to write my goals in the present tense as if they have already been achieved. This makes them seem more real and urgent. A SMART goal in this case could be:

I have increased the net, after-tax value of my business to my personal estate by $1 million to a total of $3 million by January 1, 20__, and I have sold it. The sale has met my personal criteria for success:

- I received sufficient cash to reward my loyal employees, family, and my favorite charity.

- I received enough cash to pay off all debts.

- I have a combination of cash and monthly payments from the company on a loan that I will hold which assures me of a steady annual income of $75,000+.

- My loan is secured with shares and I have retained full control of the company until the loan has been paid off.

- My key employees have been protected by a contract that assures them of employment for at least 12 months.

- The company name will remain the same until I have received full payment from the loan, and the intent is to keep the name going forward.

- I have achieved this with the support and encouragement of my advisors, employees, management team, and family.

There are, of course, challenges to this goal, as well as strategies you'll have to implement, but now you have a starting point for moving forward in a focused way toward your envisioned lifestyle, using your business as a tool for creating personal wealth.

As apparent as this strategy may seem, many entrepreneurs haven't taken this step.

6. The Benefits of Reaching Your Goal

Creating a goal is a SMART start, but then we must go beyond the statement and determine what you need to do in order to make the goal a reality.

The first step is to figure out what's in it for you. What are the benefits you'll accrue by reaching this specific goal? This creates the motivation, drive, and persistence you're going to need to spur you on through the difficult decisions, tough negotiations, and hard work that lie ahead of you.

Using the previous goal as an example, let's ask what the specific benefits of increasing the net by $1 million are? Think, articulate, and write your benefits down. Having concrete, recorded points to refer to in the future will help keep you on track.

There could be myriad benefits, including:

- The ability to pay bonuses to all my loyal staff, especially those who worked hard to make the business more successful in preparation for selling it. This is fair and will make feel good about looking after my employees.

- Enough money to be able to give each of my kids a down payment on cottages close to our family cottage.

- The ability to create an education fund for each of my grandchildren so they have the benefit of learning at a good university — probably the most important gift for future generations.

- Money to enable my spouse and me to travel the world whenever and wherever we want.

- Cash flow for continuing to enjoy the health club and its programs so we stay in good shape.

- Peace of mind, knowing that we won't have to worry about running out of money when we can no longer earn it ourselves, no matter how many years we live.

- A sense of accomplishment. It will just make me feel good about myself.

- A feeling of vindication. I will have proven to my spouse that all the late nights, the struggles, and the line of credit on the house have indeed been worth it — that we turned a challenging situation into a very positive ending.

- A sense of pride. I will be able to hold my head up and feel proud of my legacy.

7. Considering the Challenges and Obstacles

Attaining the extra $1 million isn't likely to come without some struggle. So the next step is to ask yourself, what possible obstacles, challenges, or issues will I run into in the pursuit of this goal?

If it isn't a stretch, you're not going to be very excited or motivated to go after the goal. It's going to require extra effort or planning or a new idea to energize you. What could get in your way?

Another way of approaching this is to ask yourself: If this is truly important to me, why don't I have it already? To continue our example, here are some things you might identify:

- The market is static. It's a big increase under the circumstances.

- My management team and employees already feel they are working too hard. I'm not sure I can convince them to put in more hours.

- My cash flow is tight. In order to grow that much I need to have more cash or credit and I'm not sure I have a convincing enough story to ask the bank for much more. My spouse would definitely flip if he thought I needed to put more money back into the company or use our house again as security for a bigger line of credit.

- My salespeople have become complacent. I don't see the spark and energy that was there when I managed the sales team. I'm not sure what the root cause of that is, but it has resulted in a flat and slightly declining revenue stream over the past five years.

- Our receivables are too far out. We have a couple at 120 days, a number at 90 days, and a majority at 45 days. This is negatively affecting our cash flow and credit.

- I am getting tired. It's been a long haul building this business over the years. I'm not sure I'm up for a big push that I have to lead.

- I haven't put any real effort up to this point in getting the business ready to sell. It's a mind shift for me. I'll have to work at it.

- I'm not confident that I'll be able to move away from the business. I'm not sure I want to. I know it's the right thing to do, but it doesn't feel right. It's my business.

- We've talked about stronger policies, procedures, and systems for years, but we are still pretty weak in those areas. They will have to be developed and completed in a timely manner and there is pushback from employees and managers when they are asked to do it.

- I know that some of the people on my leadership team are not A-list players. Frankly, if I were buying the company today, I would see them as a liability, not an asset. I'll have to deal with that.

- I don't know much about the tax or legal side of selling a business. How much money will I need in order to net out at $3 million? What can I expect to pay in fees?

- I'm not sure how realistic the goal is. I've never had the business valued. My preferred timing may not coincide with the market or the right buyer.

- It all feels too overwhelming. It's complex. I'm not sure I can find my way through the maze.

7.1 Solutions to potential obstacles

Obstacles aren't new to you. You've been dealing with and overcoming them all of your life, and at elevated and accelerated levels as your business grew. You know there are solutions for almost every hurdle. What are some possible solutions to those challenges we listed? Here are several to get you thinking.

- Is the market as static as I think? I need to get a better handle on the market. Is there anyone in our industry who is growing? What are they doing differently? Who are my competitors? Have any of them taken a different approach? Could I grow through acquisition? I need to make a list and analyze it to see who might be interested in selling or merging.

- If my employees are working too hard, why? Are they working smart? Are they disorganized? Are they ineffective? Do they lack creativity and initiative? Conduct a couple of employee assessments to determine what they are all feeling in a measurable way versus anecdotes. Maybe it is just a noisy few concerned about working too hard. I need to assess whether I have the right people working here. Maybe some of them need to move on.

- Cash flow has always been a problem as we've grown. It's not going to get easier, but we have to grow anyway. I need to create a better story for a prospective buyer so I might as well practice on the bankers. Even if they don't give me more money, I'll learn what they are looking for. That will give me insights for selling the business as well.

- My salespeople need a bit of a shake-up. I need to fire my sales manager in Phoenix. I think we have a few others who are just riding their renewals and spending too much time in the coffee shop. We haven't done any serious training for years. Find someone who can train and motivate my team for the next three years.

- Receivables are a little slow because our invoicing is slow. We need to get invoices out the same or next day instead of a week or two later. Speak to our GM and set some measurable standards. Ask for a weekly report on invoices compared to when the work was done, and the number of days from the time the invoice was sent to when we received payment. Then start pushing for more timely payments.

- I think I'm tired because I've lost some of my enthusiasm for the business. Just going through this process is getting me energized again, but I also need to get more physically fit. Join the gym, lose 25 pounds, and get back into playing tennis.

8. Action Steps: Things to Do, with Timelines

Now we need to look at the specifics. Call it what you like — action steps; tasks; things to do — but this is where the rubber hits the road. This is what you have to do in order to achieve your goal. Use Worksheet 4 (available on the downloadable forms kit; see the back of the book for instructions for accessing it).

Many of the sample suggestions here could go right into your plan, but you have to adapt, add, delete, and reconfigure it to make it your OWN plan. Use this thought process and template to set your goal and outline what you have to do to achieve it. Then you can work through different scenarios to see which one will provide you with optimum results.

There are two reasons why your past advisors in any given areas may not be the best people for taking you to the next step to transition or sell your business.

First, they may have no experience or interest in the specialized area of business sales or transition.

Second, they may have a vested interest in stalling or preventing you from selling your business. They may think that once you've sold it, you won't need them anymore and the fees they were receiving from you or your company will grind to a halt. No professionals would admit to that even to themselves, but it's a possibility you have to seriously consider. It does happen.

If you feel resistance from them to help you achieve your goals, assess whether they are capable and willing to do what is necessary to provide you with the best advice and results to meet your needs. If you believe they aren't, find people who are. It might lead to an awkward conversation, but this is an area in which you need to be sure you have the right team to help you make this happen.

9. Is It Worth It?

At the end of each goal-setting exercise such as what's in Worksheet 4, close it off by answering a commitment question. Once you have defined and understood the goal and listed its benefits, the obstacles to achieving it, the solutions to those obstacles, and the actions required, you have to ask: "Is it worth it? Do the benefits of reaching the goal outweigh the blood, sweat, and tears I have to go through to get there? Am I committed to doing whatever it takes to make this goal a reality? Yes or no?" ("Maybe" is not an option.)

At this point, you may answer that it isn't worth it; you're not ready to commit because the cost is too high. But if you say that it is, you are committing yourself to move forward to reach the goal. You've set yourself on a path. It doesn't mean you're unconditionally stuck with your decision. However, committing to the goal will keep you on the path if you become discouraged or distracted or lack focus. Don't get off the path without a conscious decision based on new information or circumstances that you hadn't anticipated. The downloadable forms kit also includes a worksheet to go over valuation of your business.

6
BUILD AN "A" TEAM OF ADVISORS

"We were working with a large business in which several family members were involved. Because there was a lot of money on the table, emotions ran high and the plan became stalled because the family members couldn't agree. The family dynamics put the brakes on a multimillion-dollar decision that would have saved more than $2 million in tax. There was no logic to the log jam, but we were prevented from moving forward."

– J.J., Financial Advisor, Estate Planner

1. Selling a Business Is Not a DIY Program: Find an Advisor

Unless you are in the business of buying and selling businesses, chances are that you're not the best person to sell your business. Could you do it on your own? Well, in theory you could also take out your own appendix but it's not recommended.

You need help. The difference between selling your business well or not could amount to millions of dollars. Why would you risk that at this stage?

This chapter will give you a better understanding of what you may not know and where you need to turn for advice. And you do need to turn to the experts.

I asked this question of everyone I interviewed about selling their business: "Who did you turn to for advice when you considered selling your company?"

The answers surprised me. Some sold it themselves but admitted in retrospect that it may have been a bad decision. Some relied primarily on their lawyer, some their accountant, and a number turned to other CEOs for consultation. About half of the people to whom I spoke used a business broker or investment banker. Almost all had a business coach they trusted and relied upon.

There are two major categories of advisors to consider in preparing your business for sale: technical and leadership. Technical advisors deal with taxation, legal, financial, and transactional issues. Leadership advisors are often referred to as dealing with "soft" issues. Ironically, soft issues can be very hard. They can make or break a deal. They include taking responsibility, setting the vision, managing growth, and dealing effectively with people and family issues. Generally speaking, you can save money on the technical side and make money on the leadership and people side.

The following sections discuss various advisors I recommend you engage on your journey.

1.1 A business transition coach

A number of advisors will play an important role in bringing your vision to life, but most will focus on their own narrow areas of expertise. A business transition coach, however, is like a general contractor who helps coordinate the process and keep you on track with your goals. He or she has no axe to grind and no specific interest in your choice of experts to do your tax work or legal contracts. He or she will provide objective, unbiased support and advice over time, helping to facilitate your business transition process.

1.2 A family business advisor

Owning a family business involves several complications that are absent in a non-family-owned business. Some people would argue that if you are the sole owner of your business and you have a family, you in effect do have a family business because your family members are always affected by what happens to you and your enterprise. But if you have family members who are also shareholders, a whole new layer of complexity arises. If they are shareholders and employees, you've got yet another layer of complexity. And if you have some family members who are engaged in the business and some who are not, there are additional dynamics to consider.

A family business advisor will understand these dynamics and have the experience and training to negotiate the often unexpected twists and turns associated with selling, transferring, or transitioning a family business.

1.3 A business-growth and leadership coach

If you want to maximize the value of your business before you sell it, or if you want to get it in shape so that it will continue to succeed without your ongoing personal attention, you may need to work with an advisor who is skilled and experienced in the people side of business. A business-growth coach will help you develop and execute the human resources plan to prepare your business for transition.

He or she will help you —

- create or revise a strategic plan, organizational chart, and action steps that will make the business evolve into what you need in order to achieve your personal goals;

- set the right people in the right roles to execute the business plan;

- develop your leadership, management, and salespeople to maximize and sustain your revenue and profitability; and

- customize metrics and tools to assess your progress and help you stay focused on your priorities.

Good business-growth coaches can add significant value to your business. They can help you do many of the things you always wanted to do but perhaps didn't get around to. Companies are fond of saying, "our people are our greatest asset." That is often true. Companies that invest in their people with training and development can turn that asset into a good sale price.

If you are still self-employed, using the definition we introduced earlier, and need to create a business that can run without your daily attention, you must invest in your people. A business growth or leadership coach can help you see a great return on that investment.

1.4 Mergers and acquisitions lawyer or attorney

It's unlikely that your regular lawyer is experienced in mergers and acquisitions (M&A), so it's critical for you to find someone who specializes in this area. Here are a few of the things to look for when establishing a relationship with an M&A lawyer:

- Demonstrated experience in handling mergers and acquisitions of businesses similar in size and nature to yours.

- Good business and people sense. He needs to understand that it's all about getting a good business deal, which doesn't always stem from confrontation. Conflict and aggression seem to be part of some lawyers' DNA. That attitude can kill a deal rather than get it signed in your favor. Find someone who can fight when necessary and collaborate when necessary in order to make the transaction work.

- Good chemistry with you. She needs to have complementary values and principles. If you want to conduct an honest, win-win deal with the buyer, you don't want an unscrupulous attorney who is willing to do anything to ratchet up the price you ultimately get for your business.

1.5 Tax lawyer

A good tax lawyer or attorney will have expertise in all areas of taxation that relate to selling your business, including corporate and personal income tax, international tax, and the taxation of trusts and estates.

Take a proactive approach to tax planning to achieve tax savings and take advantage of deferrals available under an increasingly complex tax system. A tax lawyer can also assist in structuring corporate acquisitions, reorganizations, and financing for corporate clients. Her primary role is to ensure that your after-tax costs are minimized and after-tax returns are maximized.

Archie in Kelowna, BC, sold his retail store and was very pleased with the process. However, he regretted that he didn't get advice to set up his wife as a shareholder in the family trust. As a result, she can't receive any income in dividends and they pay a lot more tax than they needed to.

1.6 Accountant

Your existing accountant could well be your best bet, if you are satisfied with his competence and ability to meet your business needs. Some accountants have more experience in selling businesses than others, though. Make sure yours has the experience to set things up in the best way possible to take advantage of tax laws. In a perfect world, you've been using an accountant to do your annual year-ends, check your bookkeeping, and provide advice along the way. The accountant should know your business well and be able to help you clean up your books and prepare a positive picture for prospective buyers.

Bob in Ohio wished he had hired a really good CFO a couple of years before he sold his business. "The new owner did and paid for his whole year's salary in less than a month by implementing some ideas that we should have done," he said.

1.7 Investment banker or business broker

You've probably never had to deal with business brokers or investment bankers in the past. They can bring tremendous levels of experience, advice, and concrete leads to help you sell your business. I would suggest that you speak with them at least five years before selling so they can give you an estimate of the current worth of your business and outline the specific actions you need to take to increase its value by the time you want to sell.

There are many advantages to using a broker or an investment banker, including:

- They will likely have a more objective view of your business's worth than you do. They therefore can help you set a more realistic price. Some sellers will tend to underestimate the value of their business, but most will overestimate, generating fewer interested parties.

- They should bring a number of prospective buyers to the table and as you now know, it is always best to have more than one person bidding for your company.

- They may be tapped into foreign buyers and investors who would never surface if you were selling the business on your own.

- They can negotiate on your behalf and be a buffer between you and the buyer. This is very helpful if you end up staying on in the business and have to work with the buyer for a prescribed period. Their objectivity also means they won't be offended by anything the buyer says about your business. The due diligence done by the buyer can be a brutal exercise if you are on the receiving end of the criticisms.

- They should have their fingers on the pulse of the economy and your industry, so they can advise you of the right time to sell.

The disadvantage to using them is the commission you will have to pay. However, a qualified professional should be able to sell your business at a higher price, which will more than cover their fee.

 Elizabeth owned a service business in Ontario that managed the books and administration for a number of charities. After many years, she grew tired of running the business and decided to sell it. She did most of the work herself but now regrets not having someone else negotiate the details. She lost a significant amount of money and ended up giving in on a number of points that could have been avoided by someone less emotionally tied to the business.

The people I interviewed who had used a business broker or investment banker to help them sell their businesses swore by them and couldn't imagine selling without their help. Those who had done it on their own didn't necessarily regret not having one, but they had no way to compare situations. They didn't know what they didn't know. They may well have left money on the table or worked much harder than they needed to in order to close the deal.

1.8 Financial advisor

Your financial advisor is an integral member of your "A" team. Her understanding of investments, insurance, and tax-preferred tools will help you manage risk in the lead-up to transitioning the business and to transferring business assets to create personal wealth.

A good financial advisor will work collaboratively with your other advisors to set up plans that will take advantage of advanced tax and insurance strategies to minimize, eliminate, or avoid taxes. For example, in some jurisdictions, if you have a net worth of $10 million, the right strategies could save a million or two in taxes for the benefit of your family or charity of your choice. With a net worth of $50 million, you could avoid or eliminate as much as $10 million more in taxes. That's enough to create a foundation, a bursary, or build a hospital wing in your name.

And it's not just about the tax. If you are leading the sprint to maximize the value of your business in preparation for its sale, what will happen if you die or become disabled before you get there? On the other hand, if you're grooming a successor to take your place, what if something happens to that person? You can reduce the financial risk to your family, your business, and your employees by having insurance in place that will see the plan through to fruition even if you or your successor are unable to do so.

2. Putting Together Your "A" Team of Advisors

The leadership and technical advisors discussed in section **1.** are the people you want on your team. When you choose the right members, you have a group of professionals with the education, experience, and skills to help you achieve your goals and prepare you and your business for transition. It isn't necessary to engage them all at once, but you don't want to choose them at the last minute either. That happens too often, throwing everyone into a state of crisis. I encourage you to take it one step at a time and approach each team member with a clear idea of what you are looking for and a set of questions you need to ask each one.

A business transition coach may be the first team member you need to engage. Depending on your timing, you may not need to speak to anyone else for the following few months. The farther off your deadline is, the more time you have to pull your team together. But if you are planning to sell in the next 12 months, you'll need to begin assembling and meeting with your whole team immediately.

The next person you choose to add will depend on a number of factors:

- How far off is your planned sale of or exit from the business?
- Are family members involved? If yes, are there immediate, apparent issues? Will those issues significantly affect other areas such as taxation, legal ownership, human resources, the management team, whether anyone else (non-family) can buy the business, retirement plans, etc.?

- Do you have a leadership/management team that you hope will run the business? Do you have a successor? How close is that person to being capable of taking over? Will others follow your successor willingly? What training, coaching, or mentoring does your successor need? Are there any immediate issues that should be addressed before going much further?

- Are there "B" and "C" players who will need to be given a chance to improve or leave, sooner rather than later?

- Are there existing or impending tax issues that you already know you need to deal with?

- Do you have investments outside the company that will give you some flexibility? Do you already have a retirement fund set up?

- Do you have insurance to minimize the risk of everything falling apart due to the death or disability of you or other key players?

- Do you have an established tax strategy to minimize, avoid, or defer taxes to you, your heirs, and your estate?

- Do you have a will, a buy-sell agreement, and a power of attorney in place in the event of your demise?

You're right. That is a lot to consider. That's why we're going to take this one step at a time and not overwhelm you with all of the things that have to be done.

How do you find these people? A referral is often the best place to start when beginning to recruit your team. Presumably you already have at least a couple of trusted advisors. Speak with them. Let them know your plans to pull a team together. Ask for the referrals. Ask them directly if they feel up to the job of helping you sell or prepare your business for sale. If not, whom would they recommend?

My wife tells me that I can beat some things to death by repeating myself. I can understand that after 45 years, that could get irritating. But certain things do need to be said more than once in order for people to really get the message. As an entrepreneur, you probably think you can do just about anything and that if you don't know how, you'll figure it out. That's how you survived in the early days when you started your business. But chances are you haven't thrived by trying to do everything yourself. Don't be tempted to take short-cuts and do things that should be delegated to a professional with many years of experience in a specific field. Don't be penny wise and pound foolish.

3. Ten Tests for Finding a Trustworthy Advisor

Following are the tests that consultant Jim Ruta recommends you administer to each advisor you are thinking of hiring. (Used with permission.)

1. The Recommendation Test: Does someone else trust them?

2. The You First Test: Will they visit you when you call? Do they make working with them convenient?

3. The Like Test: Unless you like them, it won't work. Trust your opinion.

4. The Plain Language Test: Unless you understand them, they can't help you. Pros make the complicated simple.

5. The Understand Me Test: If they don't work with people like you, they won't "get it." Do they ask many questions?

6. The Focus Test: Unless they specialize you won't get top advice. No advisor can do it all.

7. The Team Test: Unless they work with an Expert Team, you won't get the best advice.

8. The Process Test: Look for a Client Connection Letter to set the ground rules on the relationship, a Business System, Smart Web Site, Testimonials, Purposeful Questionnaires and brochures? Are they invested in their business and your service?

9. The Communication Test: Be sure you see them at least once a year and hear from them quarterly, as you need them.

10. The Action Bias Test: Are they prepared, passionate to help and ready to work?

Fill out Worksheet 6 on advisors, available on the downloadable forms kit.

7
WORK ON THE BUSINESS, NOT IN THE BUSINESS

The concept of working on your business, not in your business probably isn't new to you. Various versions of this message have come from Stephen Covey, Michael Gerber, Dan Sullivan, Caroline Rowan, and many others. If you've heeded their advice, congratulations! This chapter will be a reminder and affirmation for you. However, if you haven't heeded their advice, there's no time like the present to get at it.

What does it mean to work on the business, not in the business? It depends on the size of your company. If you have five employees, your list will be different from another business owner who has 500, or vice versa. But here is a sample comparison.

Early in the life of your business, you probably did 100 percent of everything. You opened in the morning and locked up at night. You sold, produced, and delivered the product and handled customer complaints. You invoiced and did the bookkeeping. You even washed the dishes and cleaned the washrooms. No wonder you didn't have time for that leadership stuff!

As time went by, you hired others to help you. That's a huge step. Your business grew, but you remained the one who knew and cared

Table 3
Working on or in the Business

Working on the Business: **Leading**	Working in the Business: **Doing**
Strategic planning either on your own or with a team of senior managers.	Setting up the strategic planning meeting. Arranging the facilitator, location, logistics …
Attending seminars, workshops, or courses on leading, growing, managing, or selling your business.	Attending seminars, workshops, or courses on software, marketing, sales, supervision, product knowledge.
Taking time to think, visualize, plan, and set goals and action steps.	Executing all the action steps yourself.
Recognizing that you need an Operations manual and a Policies and Procedures manual, and delegating the task of creating them with clear expectations.	Writing the manuals.
Attending a meeting with your senior managers and asking intelligent, probing questions. Planning what you want to get out of the meeting and assessing the value afterwards.	Calling the meeting, setting the agenda, and running the meeting.
Working with managers/supervisors to establish standards of operations, expectations, and quality controls.	Being the person who has to give the quality a pass or fail.
Communicating the vision, the mission, the goals, and expectations.	Converting the vision, the mission, and the goals into departmental objectives and performance expectations.
Meeting with advisors who can help grow/sell your business.	Meeting with product/service suppliers.
Strategic activities	**Tactical activities**

Table 3 – Continued

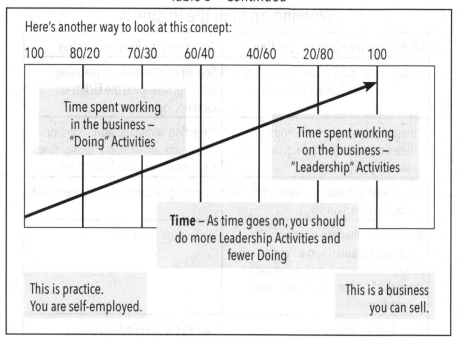

Here's another way to look at this concept:

100   80/20   70/30   60/40   40/60   20/80   100

Time spent working in the business – "Doing" Activities

Time spent working on the business – "Leadership" Activities

Time – As time goes on, you should do more Leadership Activities and fewer Doing

This is practice. You are self-employed.

This is a business you can sell.

more about it than anyone else, so you still did everything that was critical to making the business successful (80 percent doing; 20 percent leading). Some entrepreneurs never get past this point. They get stuck. If you're at this level, your business has little or no value to anyone else unless they can have you as part of the deal.

A few years ago I was a member of a CEO peer group that met monthly. Each month we would have a different speaker share ideas that were meant to help our business. One time the speaker started out by asking the question: "How many of you here are business owners?" We all puffed out our chests and raised our hands. Then he asked, "How many of you could go on vacation for six weeks or more and not worry about being away from your business?" I was the only one with my hand still up. In fact I was in the process of planning a six-month sabbatical. He went on to say, "If your business cannot run without you there, you are self-employed, NOT a business owner." With that as a clear distinction, many in the room had to admit to being self-employed.

The problem is the mindset of the entrepreneur. Most entrepreneurs don't start a business to become senior executives in a big firm.

They set up their own business so they can do what they love without the interference of a boss. They believe they know how to run the business better than any person for whom they might work.

So a frustrated mechanic opens his own auto shop. A frustrated printer starts his own printing firm. A frustrated insurance agent opens her own brokerage. A talented graphic designer starts her own agency. Typically, they are not thinking that one day they will have 50 or 500 people working for them and they will be working on the business, not in the business. In reality, they like to work in the business. They excel at it, they receive kudos for doing a great job, and it's often their efforts and passion that bring sales in the door.

You were probably one of these people and perhaps still are. If so, you have provided well for your family while doing what you like to do. In a sense, who could ask for more? Well, you could and should, because it will make it harder to sell your company if you are going to remain attached to it. Remember: If your company cannot run without you, you are self-employed, not a business owner.

The real question then becomes whether you have the time, the ability, the stamina, and the will to transform your self-employed practice into a genuine business. Are you ready to work on the business over the next few years to prepare it to attract a buyer who is willing to compensate you for what you have built?

If we consider the economic reasons for doing this, it makes undeniable sense. Winding down your company and closing it may end up costing you money instead of providing you with a payoff for all of your years of hard work. A half-hearted attempt to sell your company might not fare much better. Hoping someone will come along with an offer while you continue to operate as you have in the past won't set you up well for retirement. A suitor might appear, or might not. The better way is to decide what you want and go after it, as you have done all of your life.

1. Can You Do More "Leading" Activities and Fewer "Doing" Activities?

Ideally, you should move yourself fully to the right side of the graph in Table 3. If you are still operating on the left side, your business depends on you to do things that you probably think only you can do.

One of the common lessons shared by those who sell their business is the recognition and acknowledgment that you are not your business and your business is not you. That's a surprise for some people who align their names, persona, and self-image too closely to their company.

> You are not your business, and your business is not you.

If you have been heading in the "right" direction on the graph, the next few years are still critical to top it up. You want your employees to take on more and more responsibility while you ease yourself out of the day-to-day operations.

More easily said than done. But it must be done if you want a business that someone will be willing to buy at any point in the future.

2. Time

Working on the business takes time. Initially you steal a few hours here and there, probably in the evenings and on weekends, and you focus on thinking and planning. You read management books, listen to audio programs, and take courses. You set goals, measure results, analyze statistics, review the plan, adjust your thinking, and make even better decisions moving forward.

You think about your team: what motivates them; what frustrates them; what gets in their way of doing the job more efficiently, effectively, and profitably; how you can reward and encourage them. You think about your processes: what's working, what's not; what needs to be changed.

You think about your brand and how you can make it stronger and more meaningful in the marketplace. You think about your distribution channels: how they use your products now; how they might use even more in the future; how they can get your products faster, with fewer errors.

And now you have even more to think about. You think about whether or not to retire: what that looks like; how it will affect your relationship with your spouse; how you will fill your days. You think about how to slow down while continuing to keep the business moving forward.

If it sounds like a full-time job, that's because it is.

2.1 Houston, we have a problem

You have many competing interests for your time. If you were to make a list of your priorities now versus what your priorities would be as you prepare your business for transition, it might look like Table 4.

Table 4
Now versus Transition

As Things Stand Now	If I'm Going to Succeed at Transitioning or Selling My Business
I need to keep my existing customers happy. I need to keep my business running smoothly, managing quality, dealing with employee issues, and making a profit.	I need more time to read books like this, take courses, and learn how to prepare my business for transition. I need more time to think, to plan, to mentally prepare for the future. I need more time to coach and mentor my key employees.
I need to show good trends in revenues, margins, profits, etc. That means I need to focus my energies on that – something I've been trying to do for the past several years. Because of my business success thus far, I've been asked to be on community boards and to be a mentor to other business owners. My family wants more of my time. I have grandchildren now. My own parents need care. I'm concerned about my health. I've gained weight, lost some of my flexibility, and tire more easily. I don't have the stamina I used to have. I need to spend more time exercising and reducing my stress.	I need time to learn, to be coached by someone who can help me find my way through the maze. I need more time to talk to my advisors. I need more time to find buyers for my company. I need more time …

Sound familiar? The time crunch is actually not a new problem. You've always had more things to do than time to do them. What has changed now is the sense of urgency. You used to have a lifetime to try to get it all done. I suppose you still have a lifetime, but ...

Here's the reality: You need to work on both sides of the chart.

When John Kotter itemized his eight steps to manage change, the first was to create a sense of urgency because we are more likely to change our behavior and act on something that is urgent. That's exactly where you are now. Even if your deadline is three to five years away, you need to start now to make the changes required to prepare yourself and your business for transition or sale. It's both essential and urgent.

"That's impossible!" You may be thinking. "I can't squeeze anything more into my day. There aren't enough hours now to do what I need to do." And you're right. There are only 24 hours in a day. You can't change the clock, but you can change what you do with the time you have available to you. We have to go back to that entrepreneurial mindset. You have to change your approach to running your business. You simply can't do everything yourself. You absolutely must delegate more.

> "So the urgent drives out the important; the future goes largely unexplored: and the capacity to act, rather than the capacity to think and imagine, becomes the sole measure of leadership." *Competing for the Future* (Harvard Business Review Press, 1996)

2.2 Essential versus time critical

To make more time for high payoff activities, Caroline Rowan, co-author of the course Results-Centred Leadership, suggests categorizing your activities as the following:

1. Essential but not time critical.

2. Essential and time critical.

3. Not essential but time critical.

4. Not essential and not time critical.

The right column of Table 4 shows activities that would fall into category 1 (essential but not time critical) if done in a timely manner.

They are essential and important but not necessarily time critical. These are activities that have to be scheduled, planned, and acted on even though you may have competing activities that are more urgent or time critical. If these are not done in a timely manner, they become category 2 (essential and time critical) activities. If you haven't done them yet, you're heading in that direction.

You will always have items in category 2. These items need to be done and they need to be done now.

At their best, these activities are energizing and exhilarating because they give you an adrenalin rush. You're focused, determined, and decisive. You accomplish a lot. (This is akin to doing all of your Christmas shopping on December 24 or getting a million-dollar proposal to the client at the eleventh hour.)

At their worst, these items represent crisis-management activities that end up being poorly completed, hurting your reputation, and damaging your bottom line. Conversely, the more time you spend doing category 1 activities, the less time you have to spend managing crises in category 2.

Category 3 activities (time critical but not essential) are usually things that others want you to do: dealing with the ringing phone; the text message asking a question; the vibrating iPhone; the meeting that was hastily called to deal with a client complaint. These are interruptions and items that could most likely be handled without any input at all from you. Ask yourself, "Who would deal with this if I were on holidays? How important is it that I handle this personally? What would happen if I didn't?"

If the negative consequences of not doing activities in category 3 would be marginal or nil, then simply stop doing them. If they do need to be done and done by you, can they all be dealt with at the end of the day so you're not interrupted right now?

Category 4 activities (not essential and not time critical) are timewasters. If you do them without any conscious thought or evaluation, they can steal a good part of your life from you. Reading trivial articles or information in newspapers, magazines, or on the Internet instead of reading something that would advance your goals is a waste of your time. Don't get me wrong. I'm a strong advocate of reading fiction and entertaining articles, books, and web pages. Setting time aside to read for recreation is great, but it shouldn't be done at a time when you should be productive. The same goes for meaningless meetings, water cooler chats, and taking phone calls that haven't been screened.

In order to make time to work on category 1 activities and work on your business, you have to abandon activities in categories 3 and 4.

If you're like most people, you really have no idea how much time you're spending or wasting on each of these categories. Yes, as a successful business owner you're better than most, but we can all find room for improvement if we look for it. And we have to. That's the only way we're going to make the time to get the essential and time-critical activities done.

The best way to really get a handle on where your time is currently spent is to keep a time log. You've probably done one in the past and been amazed at how revealing it can be.

Once you see where you are spending your time, you will see where you can free more time. Begin to invest it immediately in category 1 activities, working on your business.

2.3 Make an appointment with yourself

Another way to make time to work on your business is to simply block off parts of your calendar. If you had an appointment with an important client, you would always make sure you arrived on time and stayed the duration. Other things would still get done. Consider yourself to be the most important client you have (because in this case, you are), and schedule regular meetings with yourself to focus on your business. Or you could block off a whole week and simply make yourself unavailable in the same way you would if you were sick or on vacation. The business won't self-destruct if you're not there for a week, no matter how vital you are.

Better yet, find a coach or join a program that will help you focus on getting your business in shape. Vistage.com (formerly The Executive Council — TEC), and StrategicCoach.com are examples of facilitated groups that focus on growing your business. These programs will help you to stay zeroed in on what's important.

2.3a The Personal Economic System

For a number of years, I was member of Dan Sullivan's Strategic Coach program. Dan is a creative genius who has helped thousands of successful individuals become even more successful. His Personal Economic System is a unique approach to addressing the challenge of finding time to work on your business. He advocates breaking your calendar into three main categories: Focus Days, Buffer Days, and Free Days. Each day represents 24 complete hours, from midnight to midnight.

On Focus Days, at least 80 percent of an average workday should be spent doing those activities that give you the highest return on your investment of time. They should include your three most productive activities: Typically those activities in which you have a real strength or where you can work on your top opportunities. On Focus days, your staff should protect you from interruptions and distractions and allow you to focus all of your concentration and energy on only those activities with a high payoff.

Buffer Days are for working on preparation activities: following up on promises and commitments; delegating to others; and expanding your capabilities. You eliminate your messes, reduce your company's dependence on you, and teach your employees how to do your job. Most of the activities related to transitioning your business would be done on these days.

Free Days are whole 24-hour blocks of time in which you do no business activities whatsoever. No phone calls, emails, reports, business reading ... nothing. This is your time to rejuvenate, build relationships outside your business, spend time with your family, re-energize, clear your mind, and establish a delineation between work and play, between work and home, and between work and you. Dan recommends that you constantly strive toward having more and more Free Days on your calendar, starting with the ones everyone is entitled to — weekends and holidays — and then moving on to more and more time for yourself when everyone else is working for you.

3. Start the Change Process

Preparing your business for transition or sale takes time — a luxury few business owners believe they have. But if you want to achieve the goals you've set, you must consciously rearrange your time. Stephen Covey uses an illustration that has become part of nearly every time-management seminar so I won't go into details here. The metaphor is if you fit the big rocks in first, you can still insert smaller stones and sand into a jar. Start with the big rocks: the important, critical activities that will lead you to your goals. You'll be surprised at how all of the other activities you used to do get picked up by someone else, or are left undone without adverse consequences.

To start a change process, you have to invoke a state of urgency in yourself, in your management team, in your advisors, and in your family.

Once you have more time to work on your business rather than in your business, what do you do next? That's what we're going to cover in the balance of this book. Worksheet 7, available on the downloadable forms kit, forces you to consider your time.

8
EFFECTIVE DELEGATION

If you want to free up your time so you can get out of the weeds and focus on the bigger issues of transitioning your business, you need someone who will begin to take on more and more of your current daily activities. Ideally that person will be or will have the potential to become your successor. For our purposes, we'll define a successor as someone who can earn the right to take on more and more of your duties and eventually assume the title.

Your success in achieving your personal and transition goals and driving change will be predicated on identifying a worthy and capable successor. Once chosen, you'll be coaching, training, and testing his or her capabilities and preparing that person to carry the baton forward.

The type of person you choose to delegate to as your successor will depend on some of the decisions you've already made:

1. Sell your business to a third party, a competitor or vendor, you'll want someone who can help you grow the business, in spite of the fact they may or may not be part of the deal when it gets sold.

2. Sell your business to your children, you'll want to groom one or more of your children to become the leader(s) and ultimate owner(s) of the company.

3. Sell your business to your employees, you'll want to choose someone the employees respect and trust to take over the role of leader. This could require additional years of preparation if none of your existing employees have the drive, interest, or skillset required to become the leader. Keep in mind that if someone hasn't become an entrepreneur by the time they are 40, they are not as likely to want the implicit risk and responsibility that comes with being an owner. Of course there are exceptions, but be careful not to assume that an employee who has been a good manager will be a good business owner.

4. Keep your business as an investment and have someone else run it, you'll want to choose someone who is respected and trusted by you, your family, your customers, and your employees.

5. Further, if you expect to continue to draw money from the business or hold a mortgage, you'll want to know that your successor is fiscally sound and will do whatever it takes to pay you in full and on time.

You will need to consider whether you choose an internal or external successor. There are pros and cons to both. Generally speaking, if you have an internal candidate who has the right stuff to be your successor, there are more advantages to grooming and mentoring that person than there are to seeking an outside candidate.

So your successor could be a relative, a long-term employee, a current vice president, someone you seek and hire or a partner.

1. Your Job Description

You probably do much of your job on autopilot, not really thinking about what skills, tactics, or activities you use to get your job done. In order to find the right successor who is capable of doing your job, freeing you up to do other things at a higher level, you need to document and quantify the role you currently play. Further, you should itemize the relationships that you take for granted but also contribute to your success. When you have a legal question, a tax question, a human resource question, or a concern about the market, whom do you call? You should introduce them to your successor.

To identify which current responsibilities should be delegated in order to free up your time, begin to track the activities, contacts, and unique talents that enable you to run your business.

2. What the Business Needs

You were the perfect person to bring the company to its present state. You did it! However, that doesn't always mean you're the best person to take it to the next level. Some entrepreneurs become a bottleneck because they want their stamp on every decision and new initiative. Others, as they approach retirement become risk averse or may choose not to invest in new technology, facility upgrades, or employee training, all of which are investments in the future, and also increase your value now.

Here is another perspective to consider. If you were to look at your business through the eyes of a prospective buyer, what characteristics would you be looking for in its next leader? What aspects of yourself are critical, and what additional attributes should your successor have? Should they be better at selling large accounts? Have more strength in marketing? Be more of a numbers person? Or more of a visionary who understands how your business fits into a bigger market opportunity? Perhaps you need someone who is more process-oriented or is good at developing teams.

It's hard to be totally objective as you answer these questions. You likely think you're pretty good at all those things. But now is the time to face the brutal truth, not your subjective view of it. This is where a 360-degree report or a frank and open discussion with people who know you well can come in handy. If you feel the need for even more specific feedback, ask those responsible for the effective running of the business — your VPs or senior managers — to offer their thoughts on the following questions:

- What do I do that you feel is critical to the success of the business and should be continued?

- What do I do that isn't critical and could be delegated, reduced, or stopped entirely?

- What do you feel should be done by the President (CEO or Owner) of the business if our company is to become more successful, but isn't getting done now?

3. An Individual or a Team?

Few things help an individual more than to place responsibility upon him, and to let him know that you trust him.

— Booker T. Washington

Consider whether your successor should be an individual or a team. While it is generally best to have someone who has the final word — the one in charge — you may wish to retain that role yourself and have a small team of individuals with different strengths continue to report to you on the bigger decisions, or for mentorship and coaching. For example:

Martin was slowly but surely pulling back from his business. He hadn't sold it yet, but it was in good shape, ready when the right opportunity arrived. In the meantime, it was growing in both revenue and profits, and he was spending less and less time in the office.

Three years earlier he had hired a high-energy manager with strong experience in growing similar businesses. Martin also had a long-term senior manager whom he trusted implicitly. Although the new manager was ambitious and wanted to be at the top of the organizational chart, Martin put him on the same level as his other senior manager and they both reported to him. He made it clear that he expected them to work together, to rely on each other, and to make their "partnership" work. They were empowered to run the business in the best way they saw fit in order to achieve the goals that were agreed to at the beginning of each new fiscal year.

Martin met with them every two weeks to review their progress on their goals, discuss the numbers for the previous two weeks, and coach them to continue to grow in their ability to run the business. He asked questions, listened, and offered suggestions if requested. But as long as they were on target, he didn't interfere in their plans. He was rewarded, as the business continued to improve when he trusted those he had placed in responsible roles to do their best.

4. Benefits and Challenges of Effective Delegation

The benefits of delegation are numerous, but will be unique to you. One entrepreneur may find it reduces her workload and enables her to focus on other activities. Another may be encouraged to leave the office earlier.

That doesn't mean that effective delegation is easy. Like anything that is worthwhile, there are challenges. Some business owners don't do it at all and many do it poorly.

Why is that? Well, we have lots of seemingly rational reasons for not delegating:

- If you want something done right, you have to do it yourself.

- My employees are already too busy. Delegating more just stresses them out.

- My employees don't have my level of knowledge or experience.

- It costs too much to make a mistake.

- I can do it faster if I do it myself.

- My employees aren't willing to accept the responsibility and be accountable.

- I enjoy doing it myself.

Do these sound familiar? We'll discuss these and the alternate thoughts later, so start thinking about how to convince yourself that delegation is necessary in spite of these rationalizations.

In addition to being plagued by these concerns about delegation, it is unlikely that you've ever received a formal lesson on how to do it. Few courses are offered on this very important topic, and even in MBA programs, one place you'd expect to learn more about delegation, it might be implied more than directly addressed.

"Effective delegation is the achievement by a manager of definite, specified results; results previously determined on the basis of a priority of needs, by empowering and motivating staff members to accomplish all or part of the specific results for which the manager has final accountability. The specific results for which the staff members are accountable are clearly delineated in advance in terms of output required and time allowed and the staff members' progress is measured continuously during the time period." (Management by Responsibility, Responsible Life Foundation, 2012.)

That's quite a mouthful! Let's break it down and consider the challenges inherent in that definition and some quick solutions.

It is the achievement by a manager of definite, specified results. That suggests you have thought about and defined the specific results that you are looking for. Often the message to the direct report is vague and hazy, not well defined. It could feel like it was dreamed up this morning in the shower, not thoughtfully considered, carefully written, or well articulated. It takes time and planning. Make time to think about what you are delegating and what the outcomes are that you wish to achieve. Write them out. Unless your successor is new, you shouldn't have to tell her how to do it — that's her job to figure it out.

Effective delegation requires clarity about results previously determined on the basis of a priority of needs. In other words, there has been a planning process involved, which has identified certain goals and expectations — end results that have been prioritized to meet the current needs of the business. Many entrepreneurs don't like the planning process, so this step is often left undone. Clarify your business goals. Consider the parts you can delegate and who can best champion that sub-goal. Explain where their piece fits into the bigger goal and how important it is in the scheme of things.

Effective delegation empowers and motivates staff members to accomplish all or part of the specific results for which the manager has final accountability. Empowering others can be difficult, especially if you have control issues. Empowerment is delegating the authority and power to someone else to accomplish a goal — a goal for which you are ultimately responsible. You give someone else the job to do, but the responsibility for the final result is still yours. That makes many leaders uncomfortable — putting their reputation and success in someone else's hands. First, choose the best people for the job. Second, train and coach them so they understand your values and expectations. Third, give them increasingly important and complex jobs making time to provide feedback — both positive and constructive — for their successes and failures.

The specific results for which the staff members are accountable are clearly delineated in advance in terms of output required and time allowed and the staff members' progress is measured continuously during the time period. Note the emphasis on clearly delineated, which suggests serious thought, discussion, and planning. Define the output required, and develop a measurable component or expectation. Finally, you communicate that he will be measured continuously, including regular feedback to indicate whether he is on the right track. Like it or not, this requires an investment of your time and effort after you've delegated the task. Handing it off and forgetting about it isn't effective delegation, it's abdication. Use a process for delegation and teach it to other leaders in the company. Even if you don't physically complete a form for each delegation (although it's a really good idea to do so) when you mentally go through the process in advance, you know you have thought about the key steps to making your delegation successful. See Worksheets 8 and 9 on the downloadable forms kit for details.

5. An Implied Contract

Whenever you delegate, you are setting up a contract or agreement between yourself and the other person. In order to be effective, the agreement should contain eight criteria. You've agreed —

- on the measurable results to be achieved;

- that he or she is responsible and accountable for producing those results;

- that it will be completed within a specific timeframe;

- on the level of authority your delegate can use to complete the goal because you have to transfer authority along with the responsibility;

- to measure performance along the way and provide feedback to let the person know how she is doing;

- that you have a role, he or she has a role, and you each accept responsibility for doing your part to achieve the results;

- what additional guidance is required; and

- what she should stop doing or delegate to someone else to free up his or her time.

"It is the nature of man to rise to greatness if greatness is expected of him."

– John Steinbeck

6. Consequences of Not Delegating Effectively

Think back. Have you delegated in the past without getting the results you expected? What went wrong? Would some of the guidelines we've just reviewed have produced a better outcome?

Perhaps you have your own standards or rules for effective delegation that have worked well in the past. Compare them with the previous suggestions and pick the ones that work best for you. The point is that you will be more effective if you follow set guidelines.

If you don't, you may be faced with broken agreements, missed targets, a frustrated successor or manager, money spent in areas you didn't authorize, opportunities missed, wasted time, unhappy customers and employees, and the list goes on. Effective delegation is a critical leadership skill, which has so many more pros than cons that it qualifies as one of the most important things you do as a business owner.

7. How Much Authority?

Robert was frustrated. He worked for an opinionated, controlling, autocratic boss named Fritz. Robert was the sales manager and in the past he had given everything to the company. He liked the business, the work, and the customers, and he had a grudging respect for Fritz, the owner of the business. But he was expected to make sales projections and budgets without knowing the past year's financials and results. He was expected to increase sales, but had no authority to invest in marketing or sales promotions without getting Fritz's approval. He felt that he was a puppet, doing only what he was told.

Should Robert have the authority to spend money without approval? How much? How could he be accountable for results without having the authority to do what was necessary to make it happen?

Robert's case isn't unusual. It's a common complaint of managers in every industry. He wanted more authority than the owner was prepared to give him. He felt that he wasn't trusted, that he held a title in name only, but was powerless to really excel in his role as sales manager. This was demoralizing for Robert.

When I talked with Fritz, Robert's manager, it became clear that he didn't trust Robert. He had made a mistake several years ago that cost the company money. Unfortunately, there had been no frank discussion about it, why it happened, how he could redeem himself after that experience, and, most important, the lessons learned. As a result, Fritz continued to treat Robert in a paternalistic manner, as if he was incapable of making important decisions independently. So, Robert learned to "live down" to Fritz's expectations. He was too old to change jobs. He shrugged his shoulder in a "why care" attitude and acted more like a privileged salesperson than a manager. Responsibility without authority is demoralizing.

7.1 Authority levels

Responsibility without clarification of authority doesn't work.

Mary had good intentions when she quietly promoted Jeff to the role of General Manager, reporting to her. She wished to provide him with the opportunity to run the business so she could spend more time with her new passion, her year-old grandson. Jeff was given responsibility for the continuing success of the business, but "continuing success" was not well defined. Other managers and supervisors were not informed of Jeff's new role because Mary wanted to see if Jeff would rise to the occasion and prove his ability before she formalized his position.

Mary was disappointed to find that sales began to drop, customer service got worse, and expenses increased causing a double whammy on the profit line. Within three months, Jeff was demoted to his former role and Mary was spending 50 hours a week at the office again. Six months later, Jeff left the company.

Effective delegation requires that the successor have —

- a clear understanding of what is expected, in specific, measurable terms;

- the authority and power to do what is necessary to achieve the goal(s) without fear of exceeding his or her authority or having decisions reversed;

- a clear understanding of what "exceeding authority" would look like and when the boss should be consulted or asked for approval;

- complete faith and support of his or her manager; and

- communication from the manager to others that the roles have changed, what the successor is now responsible for, and how the lines of reporting have changed on the organizational chart.

7.2 Four levels of authority

There are four levels of authority that can be given to a successor depending on the current level of their experience and skill, and the current level of confidence the owner has in the successor:

1. **Just do it.** There's no need to ask for permission, get approval, or even report on it. The successor can just get it done.

2. **Do it and report.** In this case, the successor is expected to keep the boss in the loop, but doesn't need to get advance approval.

3. **Do it only after discussion.** The successor should consult with the boss and get the boss's opinions or advice, but in the end, the successor is responsible for making the final decision without interference from the boss.

4. **Do it only after approval.** The successor should present her manager with the situation, outline alternative solutions based on her research, and then make recommendations based on her best rationale for moving forward. The manager then approves, disapproves, or requests additional information. The successor does not move forward until the manager says so.

It may be impossible to list all future decisions and how to deal with them, but if you start with common situations you know will arise and categorize them in this way, you will teach your successor what you expect and how to handle those decisions. As your successor gains more experience and you've discussed various choices and your rationale, you should be able to give more and more authority to simply act and report or just do it. If your successor has been doing the job for two or three years and you still have a lot of decisions that are "do it only after discussion or approval," then you either have the wrong successor, or you're not letting go the way you should.

8. Who's Responsible for the End Result?

Suppose you have delegated the job of preparing your business for sale. You've set a goal, set a date, selected your successor, given her

Table 5
Levels of Authority

1. Just Do It	2. Do It and Report	3. Do It Only after Discussion	4. Do It Only after Approval
Full authority	**Some Authority**	**No Authority**	

Some examples:

Business Decisions	Level
Purchase office items that cost less than $1,000.	1
Purchase equipment that's necessary to keep jobs flowing smoothly and costs less than $5,000.	2
Purchase equipment that is new and unproven but is reported to increase productivity of workers and save money in the future. Costs between $5,000 and $25,000.	3
Hire a new sales manager.	4
Fire a recently employed worker with cause.	2
Fire a long-term employee.	4
Decide on a national marketing campaign that will cost $200,000.	4
Use a temp agency to hire a part-time assistant.	3

the job, and you've begun to pull back and take more time off. Who is now responsible for making it happen?

You might say she is and you'd be right.

You might say you are and again you'd be right. The fact is you are both 100 percent responsible for the end result you have established together. Not 50 percent each, but you are totally responsible for the successful completion and so is she.

That may be a difficult concept to grasp; that more than one person can bear all of the responsibility, but if you see it as 50/50, you leave room for excuses, rationalizations, and failure.

Why is your successor 100 percent responsible? Because you have effectively delegated that responsibility to her and she's accepted it.

She now has a job to do and it's up to her to get it done. Period. No excuses.

Why are you still 100 percent responsible? Because it is still your company. Your butt remains on the line with the bank, the tax people, the employees and your spouse. If it doesn't get done, you are the one who suffers the greater consequences.

Therefore, you each have a role to play in the successful achievement of the project. When you delegate, list what you're responsible for and what your successor is responsible for when you both agree to do your part in producing the end result.

Even if you have identified people you like and believe are capable of accepting greater responsibilities or becoming your successor, it doesn't mean they will eagerly accept the increased job responsibilities. You may have to sell them on the benefits of accepting the role. As such, you become a mixture of salesperson — selling them on the job — and screener, asking the tough questions to uncover any reason they should not be considered. In either case, as taught in Sales 101, a benefit isn't a benefit if the prospect doesn't want it. What you see as a benefit could potentially be a negative to someone else. So ask them what they want and need in order to feel good about their role in the company.

9. Delegation Is Key to Business Success

Finding and grooming a successor is the number one job of a CEO. It's not easy. It's not necessarily fun. But it can be incredibly rewarding if you do it right. In the early days of your business, delegation enabled you to grow and to share some of the work with others. It was important that you do it well then, but it is critical that you do it well now. It is probably the most important management activity you undertake at this stage of preparing your business for transition.

Do it well and you are better able to sleep at night knowing you have the right person leading your team. Do it poorly and it could cost you your company.

9
CREATE A BUSINESS PLAN FOR TRANSITION

 Like most entrepreneurs, John is heavily invested in his own business. He also invested, for diversity, in mutual funds that lost nearly 50 percent of their value in 2008. While he has no control over the market, he does have time to take greater control of the value of his own business.

Many business owners like John are looking for ways to maximize the value of their businesses in order to offset losses in other areas and carry themselves through retirement. The COVID-19 crisis of 2020 was another hit for entrepreneurs — especially those living close to the wire — and many will never recover..

1. Where Are You Going?

A ship without a clear destination and map will drift wherever the tides and winds take it. The same is true of a business. A business plan is what keeps it from drifting. When you follow a business plan that produces results and shows positive projections for the future, you add significant value to your company now and for the time when you want to sell it. Your adherence to this plan demonstrates that you know your business and have predictable patterns of success.

It indicates that you have taken time to think about your operation and all of the factors that go into making and keeping it strong.

Indeed, business planning should be undertaken on a regular basis: when you are starting your business, growing it, maintaining it, and preparing it for sale. A business plan is a living document; always in flux and in need of regular updates.

Dr. Kit Silcox, in his Milestones Retreat program, provides a detailed, step-by-step guide to help business owners and CEOs set up their organizations to succeed with a strategic business plan. Such a plan is far more than a spreadsheet with numbers that you take to the bank for financing. It's an ongoing support prompting you to think about where you are, where you want to be, and how you will get there. It's a meticulous look at the factors that you need to put in place to grow the value of your business. A solid business plan answers the What, Where, When, and Why questions. Within that, the succession plan answers the Who and How.

According to Dr. Silcox, a good business plan covers at least 12 topics:

1. **SWOT Analysis:** This identifies where the organization's greatest strengths meet its most important opportunities, as well as where its weaknesses and threats overlap.

2. **Values:** The underlying principles that direct the organization's behavior in its dealings with customers, employees, and other stakeholders.

3. **Mission:** A very brief passage describing what business you are in. It serves as an affirmation for the organization.

4. **Vision:** A description of the organization in the future.

5. **Strategy:** A statement of how the organization will get to the future, with an outline of the performance targets necessary to achieve the strategy.

6. **Market Strategy:** A description of the primary client groups of the future organization as well as of the products (goods and services) that will be offered to them.

7. **Organizational Development Strategy:** The processes and systems within the organization that must change in order for the strategy to unfold.

8. **Priority Goals and Champions:** Statements of specific measurable results to be achieved in the next 12 months. Assigned "champions" provide the leadership and accountability for success.

9. **Communication Plan:** A description of how everyone will be informed about the strategy, how it is expected to unfold, and how they will benefit as it does unfold.

10. **Success Plan:** A description of how each major goal will be accomplished. It includes a definitive statement of the goal, the benefits, the milestones (mini-goals) that will occur on the journey, and the manner in which results will be measured.

11. **Strategy Action Plans:** Statements of the actions that will be taken, week by week, in order to follow the plan and accomplish each goal.

12. **Periodic Success Report:** A single page in which the champions can report their progress in carrying out their success plans.

2. Hire a Facilitator

Though you can do it yourself, a business plan will be more complete, more meaningful, and more likely to be acted on if you have a skilled facilitator work with you to —

- challenge you when you want to avoid or gloss over important issues,
- push you when you get stuck,
- support you when you get discouraged,
- brainstorm with you when you need fresh ideas, and
- help you be accountable for implementation.

As a certified facilitator of Milestones Retreat, I've helped many go through the process. Still, when I work on updating or making major changes to my own business plan, I call in the master himself to help me out and give me perspective. Fortunately for me, Kit Silcox, the creator of Milestones Retreat loves to come to my cottage for just such occasions and we share invaluable time together. I can personally vouch for the incredible power of a process that helps you go through the steps of formulating a business plan.

 One of my clients is a mom-and-pop kitchen-design business that had grown into a profitable company with four retail outlets, two sales channels, and some real-estate holdings, all of which they hoped their son and daughter would one day carry on. The founders were uncertain what to do next, believing that the business had to get bigger in order to support three families instead of one.

Proceeding through Milestones Retreat, the four family members set goals to expand the business, get more locations, and grow through the acquisition of other retail outlets. Initially, they were excited and enthusiastic. I could see that they felt they were finally making headway. Then they went through the goals, obstacles, solutions, and the necessary steps required to make it work.

But one day they woke up and had a collective epiphany. Mom and Dad didn't want to work that hard and neither did the kids. Expansion and growth was the original and obvious choice in their minds before the business plan was put on paper. Once they had written it, considered the implications, and compared it against their own strengths, interests, and personal goals, they realized their mistake. They were heading down a path they thought everyone wanted but which they had never actually discussed in an open, nonthreatening way.

In the end, they sold two locations, reduced the staff, increased their margins, and put more cash and energy into expanding their real-estate holdings. And they've never been happier. Had they continued with their original and abstract plan to expand, it could have destroyed not only the family's financial but also its emotional equity.

3. What Do You Want?

In the GYLOAR discussion (Chapter 4), you took a hard look at your ideal lifestyle. You analyzed what is important to you and you determined the various elements that will help you get what you want.

Now it's time for you to set up your business plan to support and dovetail with your personal goals. You'll want to begin living your preferred lifestyle now with a longer-term view of financial stability in your older years.

Before creating your business plan, answer these questions:

- How does my business currently support my personal lifestyle goals?

- How does my business currently create barriers to what I really want?

- What needs to change for me to get more of what I want, and less of what I don't want?

- How will a business plan help me increase the value of my business and at the same time make it easier for someone else to carry it on?

- Will I need to start a new business plan or do I have one I can dust off and update? Does the old one take my current needs into account?

- Who can facilitate me and my managers through the process to make certain we do it well? While I might be tempted to do it on my own, why would I risk shortchanging such an important step?

- How much personal income do I require in the next few years to meet my goals? What is the best way to pull that amount out of the business with the least amount of tax?

- If I plan to sell, what selling price do I need in order to reach my longer-term goals? What is my strategy for assessing current value and what I need to do to bridge the gap?

- If I sell the business, is it likely that I will have to take back a mortgage or loan from the buyer? How will that affect my income? How much risk does that entail? How can I minimize the risk? Do I need to take out buy-sell insurance on the new buyer in case he or she dies before paying me off?

- Do I want to keep some of the shares in the company for my family members or myself for a future payoff? If so, how many?

- How does my intention to transition away from the business or sell it affect the business plan? How does it affect the organizational chart? Who will take my place and manage the business while I'm working on the business instead of in it?

4. A More Nuanced Look at Succession Planning

In the introduction, I defined succession planning as the process of putting the right people in the right roles and developing a system of training, mentoring, and preparing others to take over the business at some time in the future. As you consider your next steps, it's a safe assumption that others in your company are considering theirs, too. How many of your senior managers are close to retirement age? How many will probably exit the company when or before you do? This creates a huge potential problem. Consider these situations:

1. Jules is the owner of a 150-employee construction firm. He's 58 and most of his trusted and senior managers are between the ages of 53 and 64. While he has a couple of younger managers, they aren't nearly ready to take over yet. They lack the maturity, experience, and training to manage the business. Jules has a number of concerns.

   He knows that he has a great management team, but they all came up through the ranks together. They are more than coworkers; they are friends. They golf together, fish together, and often meet socially along with their spouses. Jules is the glue that keeps them together. Like the patriarch of a family, he has their respect and loyalty. But he doesn't think they will all stay in the business if he isn't there. The business would collapse if several or all of them left.

   Without the senior team, the business isn't worth nearly as much to a buyer. They are the ones who have the client relationships and the collective wisdom that makes the company successful.

   Jules feels as if he's headed down the Niagara River toward the falls. He knows what lies ahead, but he feels powerless to do anything about it. How can he possibly replace all of the experience and knowledge locked up in the heads of his top team? It seems like an impossible task.

2. Jack owns a foundry that his father started. He and his older brother took it over but then his brother died of a heart attack, leaving Jack to carry on. He's done a great job. However, now that he's approaching retirement, he wants his daughter Sarah to keep the business going.

   Sarah is a willing and capable participant in this plan and is preparing herself for the challenge. The problem is that most of Jack's key people, who were named managers only recently, aren't that much younger than Jack. They have worked in a largely autocratic environment where he made all the decisions. Sarah won't have the same level of authority and respect that her father has and she certainly won't have the experience to make all the decisions.

Jack needs to dramatically change the way his business is run if he wants Sarah to be successful.

3. Mohammed has steadily expanded his engineering business. He grew it from a staff of one (himself) to 130 employees and over the years has invited ten of his senior engineers to become partners in the firm. "Partner" is synonymous with "division manager," but each partner is still expected to maintain his or her full load of billable hours. In the parlance of the previous chapter, they are still acting as doers rather than leaders.

The whole company is underperforming and losing profits in spite of the fact that they continue to win business and everyone is overworked and underpaid. All of the partners are in their mid to late 50s. They are beginning to realize that there has to be a better way, but they have fewer and fewer years to figure it out before they retire or die from stress and overwork.

Furthermore, the business model isn't sustainable. Bright up-and-comers are encouraged to apply for partnerships, but there are no takers. They see that it's a dysfunctional way to run a business and a life. Mohammed's fervent hope that he will sell his shares to new partners for a significant sum is diminishing.

4. Marie bought her father's industrial-supply business 15 years ago. Since that time, she has – through the force of her personality and her street smarts – grown it into a very profitable business with revenues close to $100 million.

Marie has repeatedly tried to find a president to run the company so she can reduce her involvement and pursue other interests, but it has been a frustrating and costly experience. Her management team is also growing frustrated with the lack of leadership at the top as she focuses on finding someone to replace her. While they earn excellent salaries, they aren't demonstrating that they have what it takes to lead the company – even though some of them would like to.

The business is stalling and Marie isn't certain what to do next.

These owners have big problems. From the outside, their businesses appear to be successful, but those on the inside know they are houses of cards waiting to fall. These individuals don't have a proper succession plan. That not only jeopardizes the ultimate value of their business when they sell it; it's preventing them from earning the profits they could have right now.

As Moulton and Fickel put it, "Organizations must take proactive steps to plan for future talent needs at all levels and implement programs designed to ensure the right people are available for the right jobs in the right places and at the right times to meet organizational requirements."

They go on to quote management guru Peter Drucker on the social implications of this challenge:

"The question of tomorrow's management is, above all, a concern of our society. Let me put it bluntly — we have reached a point where we simply will not be able to tolerate as a country, as a society, as a government, the danger that any one of our major companies will decline or collapse because it has not made adequate provisions for management succession." (*Executive Development: Preparing for the 21st Century*, Oxford University Press, 1993.)

Drucker must have had a crystal ball! Just recall the annihilation of portfolios and company valuations in the last recession and you'll have a sneak preview of what may be yet to come.

William J. Rothwell cites research showing that "firms in which the CEO has a specific successor in mind are more profitable than those in which no specific successor has been identified. A possible reason is that selecting a successor could be viewed as a favorable general signal about the presence and development of high-quality top management." (*Effective Succession Planning*, Amacom, 2013.)

Here's something to think about: If 71 percent of today's business owners are planning to retire within the next ten years, and only a small percentage have a plan, what will happen to our economy and our society if we don't somehow circumvent that statistic? If literally trillions of dollars change hands and yet the profitability and value of a company is left to chance (i.e., there is no plan), mercenary buyers will be able to pillage at will.

It all comes down to this formula:

Motivated Seller + Business Plan + Succession Plan + Time to Execute = More $

Consider whether the following line of logic makes sense.

1. I plan to sell my business in the next X years and wish to receive the highest valuation I can.

2. Companies with a succession plan and an identified successor make more profits now and because they are on balance better managed, are worth more to a potential buyer in the future.

3. In order to achieve the highest valuation, I also have to maximize my profits now, showing a positive upward trend. Hmm, not a bad thing: more profits now and more value in the future. I like that combination.

4. Ergo, I should develop a succession plan and choose a successor in order to meet my goals.

Yes, it may seem simplistic, but sometimes blindingly obvious conclusions are hidden from us because we can't see the forest for the trees. But if we look up, we might see the vultures circling overhead.

Many large companies do have succession plans in place not only for CEOs but for all key positions. It is the responsibility of a board of directors to ensure an organization's continuity and sustainability, and the leadership team is the driving force that implements corporate goals. If for some reason key players on that team are no longer there, that impacts the company's performance and shareholder value.

Large companies have mandates, but they also have the luxury of consultants, staff, and experts to develop succession plans. Smaller companies, whose continuity and sustainability depends even more on their leadership teams, typically have no plan at all.

Consider Figure 5 and answer the questions that follow.

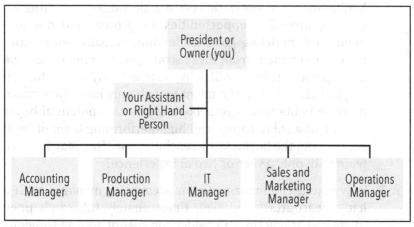

Figure 5: Organizational Chart

1. Since the early 2000s, the world was preparing for a possible pandemic. As it turns out, most didn't plan very well. When it hit in 2020 it was devastating. Almost all businesses were closed for a period and some will never reopen. If you're reading this now, maybe you survived. Congratulations! Maybe it's because you've already done many of the actions we've suggested. Maybe you and your people worked your tails off. Maybe it was luck. That whole situation reinforced the importance of succession planning. What plans do you have in place now to continue your business in the wake of this crisis and the next one that could be just around the corner? This question shows the ongoing and vital need for cross-training and preparation for sudden, unexpected, and unpredictable events. Virtually every position in your company should have a back-up so that you can continue to fulfill your promises to your clients and customers despite any setback, from illness to a fire to a strike. This need could be mitigated somewhat by having documented systems in place so that other employees could step in and follow directions laid out in a logical way by existing employees or managers. But still, how well would your business run if you lost 50 percent of your team?

2. What would happen to your sales projections, and more importantly your revenue, if your sales and marketing manager was recruited by your competitor? What would it cost you to replace her? Who is groomed to take her place? You could potentially avoid this very costly and disruptive situation by having regular, open communications with the manager, understanding her motivations and expectations, coaching for success, providing opportunities for growth and development, and modeling good leadership. Actually, your entire team could benefit from these strategies. Striving to become an employer of choice will help you to not only attract top talent, but also to keep the talent you already have. How much more valuable would your business be to a potential buyer if you had a solid, happy, and high-performing team of leaders who ran the business successfully year after year versus a team with only a year or two of experience?

3. How would you manage if your accounting manager or CFO had a heart attack and died? Unfortunately, this can happen to anyone at any time. Consider the cost of getting someone

to replace any one of your key people especially at the most inopportune time, such as the month before tax deadlines or in the midst of important negotiations with a major supplier. Are others in the department capable of carrying on the essential activities and getting the required results? Do you have life and disability insurance in place to offset the costs of replacing your key people?

4. Who would step in to advance the department if your IT person no longer kept up to date with current technology and was unable to deliver on his key performance indicators? Any individuals who have lost their motivation to stay current on trends, best practices, and emerging technology can handicap a company. Often these people will argue that the old ways of doing things worked just fine. As difficult as it is, some individuals need to be weeded out. Even if they have been loyal in the past, if they choose not to stay on top of things, they can become a liability to the rest of the team. However, if leadership is complacent, hasn't groomed a replacement, and has no plan to make changes, both the complacent individual and the company are more likely to procrastinate and not do what should be done to move forward. As the saying goes, a chain is only as strong as its weakest link.

5. Who is capable of running the business in your absence? All of the above scenarios also apply to you. What if you get sick or die? What if you no longer find working in your own company to be invigorating or in your best long-term interests? What if you lose your motivation to stay current?

Many companies that barely break even or look like the walking wounded are the result of an owner who has lost hope and confidence in the future, or has lost interest in continuing to run a business that at one time was an all-consuming passion.

These questions, while not extensive, give you a very basic introduction to why succession planning is critical. While preparing the business to run without you is important, it's not merely about you. It's about the sustainability and survival of the organization.

It's about maximizing profits today and the value of the business to a potential buyer tomorrow. It's about bringing together an "A" team of high-performing and high-potential players who can help you get what you want while you help them get what they want.

5. Practices

As Rothwell puts it in *Effective Succession Planning* (Amacom, 2013), key best practices in succession planning include these steps:

1. Using a "big picture roadmap or model" to guide the effort.

2. Ensuring hands-on involvement by the CEO and other senior leaders.

3. Using competency models to clarify what type of talent the organization's leaders want to build.

4. Developing and implementing an effective performance-management system.

5. Leading the target by clarifying what competencies will be needed for the future if the organization is to achieve its strategic objectives.

6. Using individual development plans to narrow developmental gaps.

7. Developing descriptions of the values and ethical standards required and assess people relative to those as well as competencies.

8. Building a viewpoint that high-potential talent is a shared resource rather than owned by specific managers.

9. Using leadership development efforts to build shared competencies needed for the future.

If you don't have a succession plan, you have a lot of work to do. Aren't you glad I suggested starting this at least three to five years before you want to transition or sell your business?

The subject and study of succession planning is extensive. Countless books have been written on this subject alone. For our purposes, I want to encourage you to make certain that you have considered and implemented processes to maximize the profitability now and share value later, when you sell your business. The next few chapters will give additional insights into the succession planning process.

See the downloadable forms kit for a worksheet dealing with your key players.

10
LEVERAGE YOUR ASSETS IN SUCCESSION PLANNING

1. Your Most Important Asset: People

You've heard company promotions announce that "people are our most important asset." You may have said it yourself. If there is any truth to that statement, then as you transition or sell your business, people — your employees — will play an integral role in running your business while you slow down or adding value to your asking price when you sell.

For that reason, and because of recent trends, succession planning is more important to you now than ever before. The time is gone when it wasn't as big an issue. In the past:

- If you lost an employee, you simply replaced him or her. The skills may not have been that specialized, so getting a new staff member up to speed wasn't a big deal.

- You could easily hire new employees — people were happy to have a job.

- Turnover was low. Once someone had a decent job, they tended to stick with it, and both employers and employees felt a deeper bond with each other.

- The rate of change wasn't significant; roles and responsibilities didn't evolve that rapidly, and neither did technology.

- Teaching new employees a mechanical or administrative process wasn't overly difficult.

- As the owner, you were young, vibrant, and energetic. You were going to live forever and because you built the business from scratch, you could step in and do anyone's job if someone wasn't there.

However, *Effective Succession Planning* (Amacom, 2013) indicates a number of trends that make succession planning more urgent today. It identifies these trends as —

1. the need for speed,

2. a seller's market for skills,

3. reduced loyalty among employers and workers,

4. the importance of intellectual capital and knowledge management,

5. the importance of values and competencies, and

6. managing a special issue: CEO succession.

Because of these trends, ignorance of which could cripple a company when things go wrong, you need to be prepared. Even at this stage — especially at this stage as you prepare your business for transition — you need a plan that will address the challenge of recruiting, selecting, hiring, training, coaching, developing, and above all, retaining great employees.

1.1 Internal bleeding

Employees go through four typical and easily identifiable stages when they join and work with a company. Assessing their engagement level and their proficiency in chart form looks like Table 6.

Q1 employees are hired and they enter the four quadrants in the upper left. They're excited. This is their first day on the job. Their shoes are shined, they put on their bravest smile, and they are ready to go. But initially, even though they might have trade or professional skills, their proficiency isn't high. They still need to find the washroom,

Table 6
Types of Employees

Q 1 – Entry Level	**Q 2 – Superstars**
• Highly engaged and motivated individuals • Keen to learn and do well • Not yet proficient, competent, or productive • Low performance • Cost you money – an investment	• Continue to be highly engaged and motivated • Have learned skills and knowledge • Have developed good habits • Proficient, competent, and productive • High performance • Always looking for ways to be better • Make you money – return on investment
Q 4 – Deadwood or Toxic Dumps	**Q3 – Falling Stars**
• Not engaged • Behind the times • Incompetent – should be terminated • Bad habits • Unproductive • Toxic – bad example to all and dragging down others • Cost you a lot of money	• No longer engaged • Stopped learning new skills and knowledge • Barely competent – not bad enough to terminate but not good enough to keep • Beginning to develop bad habits • Not as productive • Make money some days, cost you on others

High Engagement / Low Engagement (left axis)

Low Proficiency ← → High Proficiency (bottom axis)

learn who's who, and understand how they can make their greatest contribution. You hope these will be your future stars, and if you have a long-term view, you hope they have the potential to work their way up through the organization. But initially, they are still untested and a cost to the organization until they become more proficient. Having too many people in this category is expensive and may indicate high turnover.

Q2: After a while, depending on their ability to learn quickly and the complexity of the job, they become both highly engaged and highly proficient. They join quadrant 2. These are your superstars. They are great. They arrive early and leave late. They more than earn their pay. They are responsible and accountable. They do whatever it takes to get their job done. They like what they do and have a passion for doing it well. This is where you make your return on investment. This group can never be too big and you want to do everything in your power to keep people in this quadrant. That doesn't mean controlling them or restricting their progress. Just the opposite. You want to train, coach, support, and promote them, and show them that you care about their professional advancement.

Q3: However, over time in most organizations, some of these people become disengaged and lose their motivation. The raise in pay they were promised didn't materialize. Their boss didn't respect them. Communications broke down. Expectations were fuzzy and they didn't get regular feedback to tell them how they were doing. They didn't get training to advance them. The mission and purpose that motivated them when they were hired have become unfocused and hard to remember. As a result, they are still proficient, but not as engaged. In fact, they have slipped almost unnoticed into quadrant 3.

Gallup's surveys with employees around the world find that just 15% are currently engaged at work – that is, psychologically invested in their job and motivated to be highly productive. Two-thirds worldwide (67%) are not engaged, putting in time but little discretionary effort at work, and 18% are actively disengaged – openly resentful that their workplace needs aren't being met. ("State of the Global Workplace," Gallup Press, 2017.)

Business or work units that score in the top quartile of their organization in employee engagement have nearly double the odds of success (based on a composite of financial, customer, retention, safety, quality, shrinkage, and absenteeism metrics) when compared with those in the bottom quartile. Those at the 99th percentile have four times the success rate of those at the first percentile. (Ibid.)

Engaged employees make it a point to show up to work and do more work – highly engaged business units realize 41% lower absenteeism and 17% higher productivity. Engaged workers also are more likely to stay with their employer.

> In organizations with high employee turnover, highly engaged business units achieve 24% lower turnover. In those with low employee turnover, the gains are even more dramatic: Highly engaged business units achieve 59% lower turnover. (Ibid.)

Quadrant 3 people earn a good income because they've been with the company for a while. They know how to play the game and how to work just hard enough to stay under the radar. But at the coffee machine and in the lunchroom, they are busy. They're recruiting people from Q1 and Q2 to their way of thinking. They say things like, "What are you so happy about? Don't you know this is a lousy place to work? Management can't be trusted. There are no career opportunities. They expect you to put your head down and just do as you're told."

Whether it's true or not doesn't matter. These disgruntled employees spend more time with your new recruits than you or your managers do. These Q3ers are toxic. They reduce morale, lower quality, forget to do machine maintenance, treat customers — inside and outside — as a nuisance, and have high absenteeism. If you have a medical or benefit plan, these people are costing you extra. They may or may not be deliberately malicious, but they are no longer an asset; they are becoming a liability.

Q4: After a while, some people just give up and slip into quadrant 4. They even stop putting on the appearance of caring. They don't take training or stay abreast of issues in their field. They get sloppy. And over time they lose their proficiency as well as their engagement. They have clearly become liabilities. Because of their tenure, they may be pulling in a high salary. They can offend and lose customers or clients. They can cause new recruits to disengage or encourage them to participate in negative or illegal behavior. They make costly mistakes without the benefit of learning any lessons in the process. They slow down meetings, reject good ideas, sabotage change initiatives, and create conflict where none is necessary. Why are they still working for you?

This is such a common phenomenon, it almost seems preordained. We describe this as "internal bleeding" because it is sometimes hard to detect, yet deadly. If you don't diagnose the problem and stop the bleeding, it could cripple or kill your business. In our work with clients, we have found that 10 to 15 percent of a company's payroll is often pure waste and could be redirected to improve the company's bottom line.

Here's an abbreviated conversation I had with Fred, age 53. Fred owned a small industrial supply company servicing the oil industry in Edmonton.

Wayne: What percentage of your people, at all levels of the company, would you guess are in quadrant 1 highly engaged, but not yet proficient and productive?

Fred: We're doing some hiring right now, so probably about 10 percent.

Wayne: What percentage would fit into Q2? Highly engaged and highly proficient?

Fred: We've had a tough year, so I think only about 25 percent.

Wayne: What about Q3? The people who are beginning to lose their edge. Those who are no longer highly engaged but can still do the job?

Fred: Unfortunately, I think that makes up the lion's share of my company. We better put down 50 percent.

Wayne: And that would leave 15 as the percentage left in Q4. Does that sound right?

Fred: Yup, that seems to add up.

Wayne: OK, now let's assume that the people who are in Q2 are earning 100 percent of what you are paying them. In other words, if you are paying them $50,000, they are worth every penny. You get full value from your salary dollars. But if the people in Q2 are worth 100 percent of their salary, what percentage of their salary do you suppose the people in Q3 are worth? Political correctness and legalities aside, how much would you drop their salaries to allow for their true value to the company?

Fred: Well they aren't nearly as good. I don't suppose they are worth any more than 70 percent of what Q2 employees are worth.

Wayne: And yet, on average they make about the same amount of income? What about Q4 people?

Fred: You've got me wondering if they're worth anything, but for sake of argument, let's say they're worth about 40 percent.

Wayne: How many employees do you have in total?

Fred: It goes up and down a little depending on the season, but let's say 100.

Wayne: OK, that makes it simple to calculate. If you took your total payroll and divided it into the number of employees you have, what would you estimate is the average income of your employees?

Fred: That's pretty easy. With 100 employees our payroll is $6.5 million, so the average is $65,000.

Wayne: Now, I'm going to let you do the calculations so we make sure we get this right. Of course, these are ballpark figures, but they give you an idea of the hidden cost of internal bleeding. Let's skip Q1 and Q2 for a moment and look at Q3. If you have 50 people who are earning an average of $65,000 but are only worth 70 percent of that because they aren't engaged, let's take 50 x $65,000 x .30 (the difference between 100 percent and 70 percent) and the answer is?

Fred: $975,000.

Wayne: Just write that number down and let's go to the next quadrant. In Q4 we take 15 people times $65,000 and multiply that by 60 percent (the difference between 100 percent and 40 percent) and the answer is … $585,000.

Wayne: Adding those two numbers together we get?

Fred: $1,560,000! Holy ****! Just a minute – that's 24 percent of my payroll!

Wayne: And if we divide that into the number of working weeks per year, let's use 50 for easy figuring, your average cost per week of having disengaged employees is?

Fred: $31,200!

Wayne: That's a scary number and just a really quick, high-level view of what it could be.

Fred: Actually, that's a little hard to believe. Are you saying I'm losing $31,000 every week – paying that out for work that isn't being done?

It gets worse. I was sharing this concept with a group one time and came up with a similar number. I asked the company comptroller, "Are we off base here? Do these numbers make sense?" He said, "I think you're actually quite conservative. You haven't factored in the additional costs of broken machinery because the employees don't care to maintain it properly, the cost of sickness, accidents, and lost time, the cost of employee theft, the loss of customers, the loss of good employees that you want to keep, the toxic environment that just drags everyone down — and that doesn't count the incredible cost of attracting, recruiting, hiring, and training a new employee when someone leaves." All I could say to that was, "Wow!" I've come to see that he is so right.

2. What's Happening in Your Company?

If we could graphically depict the number of people in Fred's organization that populate each quadrant, it might look like Figure 6. You can immediately see that Fred has a problem.

If Figure 7 is representative of your company, you have something to sell. The bulk of your people are highly engaged and highly proficient. They are worth something to a prospective buyer and they are capable of running your business whether or not you are there. You have a few people in the other quadrants, but that's not unusual and can be addressed fairly easily.

The Figure 8 illustration is a picture of a mature business that has a problem with turnover. Some of the trouble here could relate to the higher number of people in Q3. The Q3 people overshadow the few stars that you have and as a result, the culture is one of mediocrity, complaining, and poor performance. New employees might be persuaded by the recruiter that they are joining a great company, but they soon learn the truth. As assets go, this company's employees are not adding value. In fact, if this company were to be purchased by an investor or competitor, most of the employees would be seen as liabilities and would be dismissed or packaged out as part of the deal. The founder of this company will be disappointed with the selling price of his or her business.

Figure 9 represents an old business that is crippled by its employees and is like the walking wounded. It has little new blood coming in, few stars, and is overwhelmed by people who are not engaged. Don't get me wrong: This isn't the employees' fault. It's a management problem and a recession will likely finish them off if they don't get bailouts from our tax dollars.

I think you get the picture. Take a few moments now to visualize your entire employee roster. Using your gut instinct, categorize them into each quadrant. How many do you have in each one? Now, imagine what your business would be like if almost all of your people were in Q2. How would that change your culture, your performance, your profitability? How would that change the value of your business when it comes time to sell?

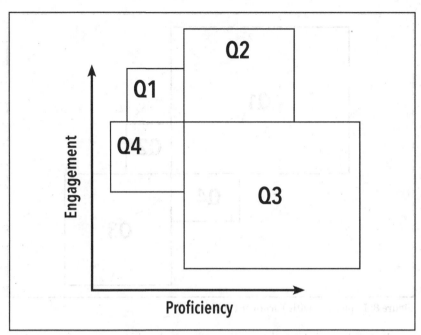

Figure 6: Fred's Quadrant Depictions

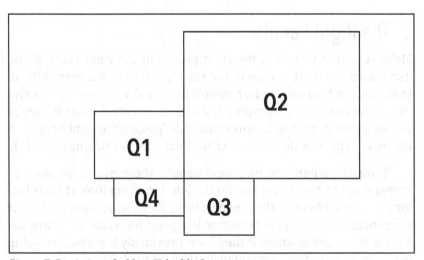

Figure 7: Depiction of a More Valuable Company

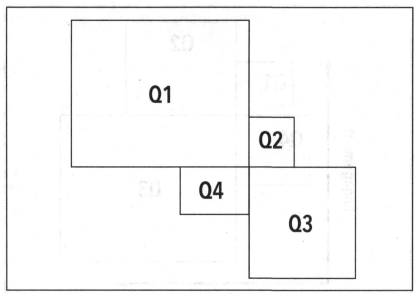

Figure 8: Depictions with Turnover Problem

If you have internal bleeding in your business and you want to stop it, I recommend that you focus on five key areas.

3. The Right People

Make sure that you have the right people in the right roles. If you don't have the right people doing the right things, it's very difficult to succeed in business. In fact, people are usually the most expensive component of an organization, but also its greatest asset if they're working effectively. Jim Collins called this "getting the right people on the bus," in his classic book *Good To Great* (Harper Business, 2001).

Typically, when you hire new people, there are three ways to assess them to see if they can do the job. First, you look at their history — their résumé, their experience, their education, and their references. Because past behavior is a good indicator of future behavior, you want to know if they have previously been successful in performing activities that you want them to perform.

Second, you look at the interview results. Did they show up on time? Are they confident? Did they respond appropriately to your questions? What is your first impression and gut feeling?

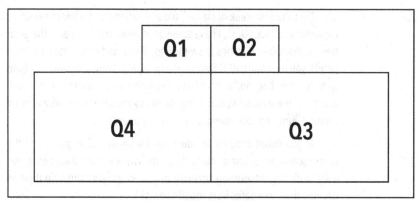

Figure 9: Quadrants Depicting Crippled Company

Third (and this is every bit as important but is often skipped by many companies in the hiring process), you look at their job fit. Do they fit the job, the team, the roles, and responsibilities? For example, just because a salesperson was successful in one job doesn't mean he can sell your products to your clients in a new territory, with your sales manager leading him. You've probably hired people who appeared right when you offered them the job but didn't turn out to be what you expected. In many cases, it was because their personality or their interests were not a good fit for the job you wanted them to do.

Have you ever hired a salesperson who couldn't sell, a manager who couldn't manage, or a leader who couldn't lead? You can't turn cabbages into oak trees. If they don't have the fit for the job, they'll never graduate to Q2. They will either quit, get fired, or slip under the radar into Q3 and Q4.

There are many assessment tools on the market today to help you in the hiring process. I highly recommend that you get as much information about an individual as you can before you invest thousands — maybe hundreds of thousands — of dollars in hiring and developing him.

4. Performance Training

The forest animals were concerned about falling behind in the changing environment so a committee was formed to set up a school. The owl was considered to be the smart one so she was nominated to become the principal. Then they set up a learning curriculum that included running, jumping, swimming, flying, burrowing, and climbing trees.

After the first week of classes, the owl called the duck into her office for some feedback. "Duck, I have some good news and bad news. The good news is that when it comes to swimming, flying, and quick stops on small ponds, you are amazing! However, your jumping, burrowing, and climbing trees is pretty bad. So, here's what we're going to do. We're going to pull you out of the swimming and flying classes so you can spend more time on running, jumping, burrowing, and climbing trees."

As you might imagine, the duck quickly became disengaged and the school soon had its first of many dropouts. While it's not always easy, you want to identify the existing strengths of your employees and help them to develop those strengths from "good to great."

Think about it. Are you trying to train introverts to become outgoing salespeople? Are you training highly creative artistic types to become better organized? Consider the personality and abilities of your employees and encourage them to maximize their strengths and minimize the negative effects of their weaknesses. For more on this subject, consider reading the series of books by Marcus Buckingham, starting with, *First Break All the Rules*.

Once you've hired the right people for the right jobs, they need training. We could divide this area into four broad categories.

First, employees need to have a good level of knowledge. Regardless of their job, whether they are in sales, engineering, accounting, or production, they need to know their products, their equipment, and how you do business. This is a basic foundation. It's their ante to get into the game.

Second, they need a good attitude. Again, it doesn't matter what job they have, their attitude is going to impact their performance, how they get along with others, and how they achieve their goals. Attitude and emotional intelligence are so important that people with incredible skills and knowledge could still be liabilities if they can't respond maturely and appropriately to situations. Many companies today are identifying a good attitude as one of the most important characteristics employees bring to the job. If they have the right attitude, their shortcomings in other areas can be managed. And yet, attitude is still a greatly misunderstood attribute. Companies are now beginning to provide training to help employees develop and maintain a good attitude.

Third, employees need certain skills in order to be effective contributors to the team. If they sell, they need selling skills. If they supervise, they need supervisory skills. If they do payroll, they need bookkeeping skills. Skills can easily be taught to people who have the right aptitude for the job.

Fourth, great employees need good habits. They need to know how to set goals, focus on priorities, do what they say they are going to do, arrive on time for meetings, plan their work, and get things done effectively and efficiently. Knowledge, attitude, skills, and habits: This is sometimes called the KASH formula, which is an appropriate name because they will bring cash into the business. Individuals with better KASH are worth more to their employers. But here's the switch: Today's employees expect their employers to provide performance training in KASH. One of the common traits of the 100 best companies to work for is their penchant for training and developing their people. If you don't offer training that is meaningful and helps employees grow and advance their careers, you are more likely to have people sliding into Q3.

You also need to continue to provide or encourage training for people in Q2 in order to groom them for greater responsibilities. You draw your candidates from this group to fill other roles in your succession planning process.

Business challenges can vary by region, but one stands out the world over: The need to prepare the workforce for the future.

When PwC released its 20th CEO survey this year, 77 percent of corporate leaders agreed skills shortages pose a threat to growth. At the same time, more than half said they planned to add new hires who will all need integration into their new roles.

This is where the "World's Best Workplaces" – recently announced by *Fortune* and Great Place to Work – offer some of the most valuable insight. These companies excel at creating agile, adaptive organizations on a global scale. And analysis of their programs found professional development was the top area separating them from their peers.

5. Great People Management

The next area is great people management. Not just good management, but great management. Here again we can divide this into four key categories. Great people managers have management KASH: management knowledge, management attitude, management skills, and management habits. They are focused on their people and resources. They have a caring, coaching instinct and love to see people grow and succeed. They know that people have unique strengths and weaknesses and they understand that their job as managers is to get the best out of their people's strengths and to minimize their weaknesses. They develop their people. They are like catalysts. They have the ability to take the vision of the organization or the visionary leader and translate it into clear goals, projects, results, and expectations. While they might be seen as leaders in their organization, I make a distinction between great people managers, and visionary leaders.

6. Visionary Leadership

Great companies need visionary leaders. Most entrepreneurs are visionary leaders as opposed to people managers. Visionary leaders are forward-looking. They still need management KASH. But they are never satisfied with the status quo. They are optimists and future-oriented. They can see the future more clearly and vividly than many people see the present. They see opportunities in the market, new ways of doing things, and new services or products to offer to their clients. They are creative, visionary, and they can get people caught up in their visions. While they do need to understand and be competent at doing the things great people managers do, that is often not their strength. Many companies — many visionary leaders — don't recognize that the two jobs are distinct, unique, and require different types of people. If you've been attempting to play both roles, you may have trouble playing either of them effectively. They both require focus and attention, but each demands a different mindset and ability.

I often see the lights come on when I discuss this perspective with a visionary leader. Many leaders feel guilt for their lack of management skills rather than pride in their visionary skills, and this discussion feels liberating to them.

7. Business Diagnostics

The final area to leverage is business intelligence or diagnostics. Information can give you more power and confidence.

How do you identify and quantify the real issues, challenges, and opportunities so you can focus your resources (time, energy, employees, and budgets) in order to produce consistent, sustainable, predictable, and profitable results? And do it economically?

You need accurate business data and diagnostics. What critical issues do great managers need to understand and focus their time on? What unique opportunities should the visionary leader be going after? What pending dangers does he or she need to avoid? What are the most important qualities we want in new recruits and how do we identify them? What are the priority performance issues that we can address with training that will ensure a return on investment?

In order to be useful and practical, business intelligence and diagnostics have to be easy to analyze; easy to act upon; easy to gather; and accurate and meaningful.

There's no point in having a thick binder filled with data that no one ever looks at because the information is too complex or doesn't point to some obvious actions. This information can be collected through research, one-on-one interviews, suggestion boxes, surveys, and assessments. Surveys and assessments are usually the least expensive and most accurate because they enable your customers, managers, and employees to speak freely and anonymously in a structured process that categorizes and quantifies the data.

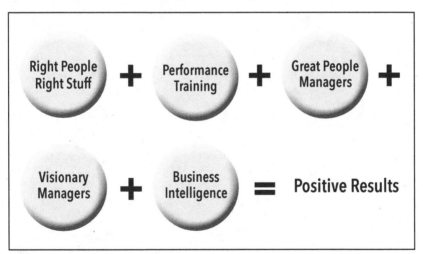

Figure 10: Five Circle Solution

I call Figure 10 the Five Circle Solution to Growing Your Business Intelligently. Add the circles together and you get bottom-line results. Take away any one of the circles, and you diminish the value of your company and the results that you are capable of achieving. What results are you looking for?

"How important were your employees in the sale of your business?" I asked Kim in Toronto.

"They were absolutely critical," he replied. "They got behind the process and as a team we strategized the whole thing. I offered them incentives based on the final price we got for the business. In the end, I bought five brand new BMWs as a thank-you for their help because they really worked hard. Your employees can make or break your deal."

See the downloadable forms kit for a worksheet dealing with your people.

11
SUCCESS IS A PROCESS

In his classic business book *The E-Myth Revisited* (Harper Business, 2004), Michael Gerber asserts that process is what differentiates successful companies from the also-rans. He says that franchises succeed because they have a clearly defined system or process for everything. They have a process for —

- hiring staff,
- advertising,
- purchasing,
- invoicing,
- greeting customers,
- banking,
- selling,
- performance reviews and coaching,
- identifying top performers,
- promotions, and even
- cleaning the washrooms.

Gerber goes on to argue that you should build processes into your business as if you are creating a franchise, even if you have no intention whatsoever of franchising it. In other words, the act of defining a process, documenting it, testing it, tweaking it, and coming up with a standard step-by-step methodology for everything in your business as if you were establishing a turnkey, repeatable, franchisable process will help your business succeed.

The alternative to managing by processes is managing by the seat of your pants. This can work if you are brilliant, creative, intuitive, and the sole owner and sole employee in the business. But as soon as you have one employee and need something done when you aren't there to supervise, you need a process. Otherwise, your customers will not have a consistent experience with your company. Most fast-food franchises are successful because of their unwaveringly predictable consistency, not because of their culinary delights.

No matter where you go to a McDonald's — in Jacksonville, Boise, Calgary, or Paris — you get exactly what you expect. The restaurant and washrooms are always clean. The staff always wear uniforms. The menu is the same, with perhaps a minor local variance. The hamburgers taste the same. (No better and no worse.) Employees all greet you exactly the same way and they always ask, "Would you like fries with that?" Think of the incredible efficiencies, performance measurements, and competitive advantages a company has when it has developed such processes and proven repeatedly — in thousands of locations — that it has mastered the best possible way to conduct its type of business.

Process is one of the main reasons that franchises are so successful. Someone buying and running a franchise is significantly more likely to still be in business three years later compared with someone starting his or her own business in a similar field. Is the franchisee more intelligent, more passionate, or more committed to success than the non-franchised competitor? Probably not, but statistically the franchisee is much more likely to succeed and earn a better living.

Why the advantage? Because franchisors have developed business processes that enable their franchisees to succeed by stringently following the tried and true. They even put processes in place to make sure the franchisee follows the processes. They have developed best practices through trial and error and arrived at an approach that works. Not only does it work, but it works every time.

Franchisors have invested the time and money to make mistakes so their franchisees don't have to.

Assuming that you are not part of a franchise, you and your staff may have some heavy lifting to do to create a business that operates as if it were a franchise. Building documented processes for each part of your business will help you —

- increase sales,

- reduce costs and expenses,

- hire the right employees,

- retain your best employees, and

- keep your customers coming back.

More importantly to you, a business that is run by systems rather than the day-to-day whims of individuals is easier to manage, easier to sell when you're ready, and worth far more to a prospective buyer.

1. Where Should You Start?

Ask yourself, your employees, and your customers this question: What is the most important part of our business that could benefit immediately from a systematic process that would assure consistently successful results?

Roll that question over in your mind. Brainstorm answers, prioritize them, and then do it. Start on the most important area: Think through the steps, document them, review them, test them, change them based on feedback, and test yet again. Once you are at the point where you are happy with the outcomes, document the process again and teach it to your employees. But don't stop there. You need to teach them again, monitor their success with the process, and repeat it until it becomes an ingrained daily routine of doing business.

Ask your salespeople the question, because they won't be shy about giving you an answer. Here are but a few of the things that you may hear:

- We set sales goals every year that are mostly meaningless. I'd like to know exactly what I need to do to reach those goals and have the information every week to know if I'm on track.

- I'd like to know exactly when the customer is going to receive his order so I can confidently tell him when to expect it.

- We want our resellers to sell more, but we have no way to help them — at least not a way that's consistent and predictable.

- We throw money into advertising but we don't track what works and what doesn't. I'd like to see a process that measures our return on advertising dollars so we can improve the number and quality of leads we get.

- We talk about working smarter, but I haven't seen a change that would indicate that we're doing that. How could we turn working smarter into a concrete reality?

Here is a tale of two salespeople: Fred, who has a proven sales process, and Eleanor, who does not. By contrasting their experience, results, and levels of confidence, we can see how a sales process can transform an average, struggling salesperson into a businessperson with a predictable income.

Both Fred and Eleanor have been in sales for about ten years. Neither is a rookie. Neither is naive about what it takes to be successful. Both work hard. Both are on commission. They work in the same industry.

But Fred makes nearly twice as much income as Eleanor, works slightly fewer hours, and is optimistic about the future. Eleanor isn't so sure selling is right for her.

Eleanor's mentor was an older salesperson who believed that selling was an art. "It's all about personality, getting to know the right people, and being charming," he often told her.

About five years ago, Fred attended a sales training program and learned that while there is an art to successful selling, there is also a science to it and a step-by-step process that can be learned, practiced, critiqued, and improved on over time. Fred's coach told him, "When selling becomes a process, it ceases to be a problem. When selling isn't a process, it's always a problem."

Eleanor prospected for new business when she had time, when her checking account was getting low, or when her sales manager got on her case.

Fred was forever prospecting and kept a daily record of how many sales appointments and service appointments he had, how many referrals he got, how many phone calls he made to set up appointments, and how much time he spent in selling activities versus administration or driving.

Eleanor had a rough idea what she would say when she met someone for the first time, but for the most part she would wing it. She felt that she would come across as more natural if her speech wasn't rehearsed, and that prospects would like her better as a result.

Fred knew exactly what he planned to say but was prepared to be flexible if it turned out not to be appropriate. He also analyzed his situations later to determine whether he needed to change his approach or change the type of prospect he was seeing.

If Eleanor went for a month without sales, she was discouraged, frustrated, and annoyed, but she had few benchmarks or statistics to compare for data, so she was unsure what she needed to change in order to improve her results.

Fred never went a month without sales. He knew at all times exactly where he stood relative to his own benchmarks. If anything was beginning to slip, his dashboard of data told him what changes he needed to make to get back on track. He knew how many new prospects, first appointments, second appointments, proposals, follow-ups, and closing appointments he had at any given time. He knew his standard and he knew if he was off track. If he was not making enough sales, he could assess his numbers and determine if he didn't have enough first appointments or if his ratios were off (the number of second appointments compared with first interviews and number of sales compared with closing interviews, etc.).

If Eleanor made the sale at the end of an appointment, she saw it as the result of everything just clicking. If she didn't get the sale, she didn't know what had gone wrong. She usually blamed it on the prospect, the economy, the poor marketing materials provided by her company, or the antiquated website her employer maintained.

At the end of each appointment, Fred had a checklist to assess if he had missed any steps, veered off track, or said things he shouldn't have said. Sometimes this checklist reminded him to go back and ask a question or cover a point he had missed, re-engaging the prospect to keep the sales process going.

When the economy slumped, Eleanor did, too. She just assumed things would simply get worse, that she had no control, and that she might as well just hunker down and ride out the storm.

Fred, on the other hand, assumed control, went back to his sales process, decided where he could work a little harder and a little smarter, and was able to keep his sales on track. A negative economy had little impact on his results.

A sales process that enables you to map out a plan, refine the plan with statistical feedback, and establish benchmarks for success will help you leverage your charming personality into a predictable revenue stream.

A friend of mine, Len, recalls one of his tasks as a young HR representative when he worked for Ford Motor Company. He was to go out to the parking lot every morning and count the number of bicycles and fax a copy of the count to Ford World Headquarters in Detroit before the daily executive meeting. Apparently, someone performed this exact routine every morning at every Ford-owned facility worldwide.

Surprisingly, no one before him had had the courage or curiosity to pose the question, "Why are we counting bicycles?" Len did. His supervisor didn't know the answer, nor did the supervisor's manager.

When they dug deeper, they learned that it had been a standard procedure when Ford was still a young company. The number of bicycles indicated to senior management how they were doing at providing an affordable means of transportation and helped them gauge what their own employees could buy and what level of wages were needed for them to be able to purchase and operate a car.

The information hadn't been looked at in years — maybe even decades — but someone was still paid to collect it every day.

All of your organization's processes should be assessed from time to time to see if they are still worth doing.

So again, ask the question; "What is the most important part of our business that could benefit immediately from a systematic process that would assure consistently successful results?"

Suppose you were to ask your IT department the systematic-process question. What about your shipping department? What about accounting, customer service, manufacturing, purchasing, janitorial, management, human resources? Each of them will tell you that they have a process, and they do. But then ask them if it's documented. Ask them if someone else could look at the documents, follow the instructions, and see the task through to completion. Ask them when they last reviewed the process in light of changes to technology, demographics, and new insights. Ask them if the process was developed through an innovative, thoughtful approach or by following the line of least resistance.

You might wonder why at this stage — when you are getting older and thinking about stepping back — you would want to invest the time, money, and energy into making your business a model of replicable franchises. If you haven't done it up to this point, why start now?

Good question. The answer will be as individual as you are, but here are a few possible reasons:

- It gives you something intelligent and purposeful to do in the next three to five years that not only will build a stronger, more viable business, but also pay huge dividends when you sell it.

- It creates a lasting legacy. If you get this right, the business can continue to run and be successful whether or not you are around to manage it.

- It diminishes the fear of not having a business worth selling or one that could actually decrease in value over the next few years.

- If you offer the business to family members or senior employees to purchase, you will feel confident that they can continue to run it successfully. And if you take back the mortgage, you are more likely to get your monthly payments.

- It provides additional security for existing employees.

- It could be a lot of fun! You might even be less inclined to sell the business once you've got it running that smoothly.

There are five further steps to take after you've asked the question:

1. Measure.

2. Improve.

3. Measure again.

4. Implement.

5. Measure some more.

1.1 Measure

How does Fred know that his system works better than Eleanor's? He measures it. He measures everything. He measures his activity statistics, his time, and his results. In his book *The Game of Work*

(Gibbs Smith, 2012), Chuck Coonradt looked at how people approached sports as opposed to work and observed an interesting phenomenon. When people are engaged in sports, they will —

- work harder,
- take greater risks,
- stay motivated even in defeat,
- endure greater pain and discomfort,
- listen more to their coach,
- go above and beyond the call of duty, and
- work harder to get along with their team.

They do all of this even though they don't get paid to do it. In fact, they actually pay for the privilege!

Chuck has been known to say, "People will pay for the privilege of working harder than they'll work when they're paid."

Think about that. At 5:30 a.m. the Saturday morning after your employees have complained about having to work in a cold office because the heat's turned down a little, they eagerly pack up their cars, drive three hours to a mountain, sit on a hard bar that is propelling them up steep cliffs in freezing weather with snow swirling around their heads, only to put their lives at risk as they plummet back down the mountain at speeds that would scare the horns off a gazelle. And when you add the cost of filling up the SUV, the rentals, and the expensive lunch, their wallets are potentially $500 lighter.

Why do they do this? There are a number of reasons, but one that Coonradt argues strongly is that games and their players are measured to the nth degree, whereas most people have no idea how they are doing at work. Ask a customer service person how she's doing, and you'll likely get a slightly confused, "OK, I think." Ask a weekend warrior on the golf links how he's doing, and he'll tell you his handicap, how many balls he lost, how many shots he took on the fourth hole, and exactly how he did compared to his buddies.

Once we get past the resistance to change and the excuse that we're too busy, we like to measure. We like to keep score. It motivates us to do better.

In one case of understated leadership, the president of a manufacturing plant made a rare appearance at a workstation and asked how many widgets they had produced on that shift. The foreman answered 750.

Without a word or indication of judgment, the president took a piece of white chalk and marked the number at eye level on the corner of the machine.

When the next foreman came in for the following shift, he noticed the number and asked his fellow worker what it meant.

"You won't believe it, but the big boss just came down, asked me how much we did on our last shift, and wrote the number down."

The second foreman thought he had better improve upon that in case the president came to ask him the same question. Which he did. "We produced 810 widgets," he reported with a crooked grin and slightly puffed chest.

The president again said nothing. He just nodded, rubbed out the first number, and replaced it with 810. A week later, the president was writing 1,100 on the machine. This management exercise took him only seconds. It required little effort and no pleading, cajoling, or yelling to get performance to improve.

You may have heard of the famous case referred to as the Hawthorne Effect. In a landmark study, consultants were assessing the effect of better lighting in a factory. To get a benchmark, they measured productivity on an assembly line. Then they raised the level of lighting and measured again. They were pleasantly surprised to see that productivity had improved. They increased the lighting levels again and measured. Productivity improved again. Smiles all around. They decreased the lighting levels back to the original setting fully expecting that productivity would revert back to its benchmark level. To their surprise, they found that productivity actually increased again.

Through further extensive tests, they determined that it was the act of measuring performance that made the difference, not the lighting levels at all.

Anything measured will tend to improve. That's human nature. Want to lose weight? All you have to do is write down everything you eat and (honestly) add up the calories every day. Want to increase sales? Measure the daily activities that lead to sales. Want to increase profits? Measure the daily factors that affect profits. The only other qualifier I would add is that the person measuring should be the one who is empowered to make the necessary changes as they are uncovered by the measurement process.

Once you have a list of areas in which you'd like to improve performance and remove ambiguity, pick the most important ones and begin to measure everything about them. For example, measure —

- the number of steps it takes to set up a new project or campaign;
- sales leads;
- ratios — leads to phone calls, phone calls to appointments, appointments to sales;
- the number of daily hits on your website;
- the number of Requests for Proposals;
- average sale sizes;
- sales of this product versus that one; red ones versus blue ones; and
- the number of sales per salesperson.

Measure, measure, measure! Revenue per employee. Revenue per manager. Number of pages of paper used per employee. (You'll be surprised and money and trees will be saved.) Amount of waste per employee shift. Number of widgets produced perfectly and pumped out the door. Whatever is important, or might lead to an insight into how a process is working now, start to measure it. Only when you have a benchmark can you take the next step.

1.2 Improve

Here's the interesting thing: If you've convinced your people to measure honestly, the improvement part is relatively easy. They won't have to be exhorted to improve; they'll want to. Your role is to encourage, support, and inspire them a little.

Help them set goals. If the benchmark is X, get them to decide how far, how fast, how much better they can do. Encourage them to innovate, get creative, and seek ways to do it better. Uncover steps that could be eliminated.

Expect some failures. They will try some things that won't work. Improvement isn't a straight line. Give them permission to fail and learn from their mistakes.

As they improve, get them to document every step in detail. What worked? Try it again. And again. If it works consistently, it may become a proven process.

But be careful that you don't stop improving too early in the process. Don't judge their new performance as good or bad. Simply ask them if they can do better.

I often facilitate a fun team game in training sessions to incorporate these ideas.

First, I get everyone to stand up and form a circle. Typically they are already around a boardroom table or U-shaped set of tables so they make their circle around the table or outside tables.

Then I toss a Nerf ball to one of them and give the following instructions: "I'd like you to toss the ball around the circle to anyone you choose, in no particular order. Just get comfortable tossing and catching the ball."

Soon the ball is going around the group, often with a few high-testosterone individuals whipping it at their buddies.

After a few minutes, I call a time-out and give these instructions: "This time I want you to toss the ball in a random pattern around the circle so that each person eventually touches it only once and it returns back to Tom here, " as I point to the person holding the ball. "But one additional instruction — remember who you passed the ball to."

Again, the ball goes flying around the room eventually returning to Tom.

"Next, I want you to keep the same pattern, " I continue. "Pass the ball to the same person you did before; have everyone participate and get it back to Tom. But this time I'm going to time you to see how long it takes. " I look down at my watch and say "Go!"

Now there's a little pressure. More concentration. The ball is more likely to be dropped this time. But that's okay. We do it, time it, and I write the number of seconds on the flip chart. In a small group, it's typically 20 to 30 seconds. We now have a benchmark. Let's say it's 30 seconds.

"Next I want you to set a goal," I say. "How quickly do you think you can get the ball back to Tom?" There's a pause and then the answers come back: "20!" "No, 18!" "Are you crazy? I say 23." A brave soul might venture "15." He or she will be pooh-poohed for being unrealistic. Without any judgment, I simply record the numbers on the chart next to the 30 benchmark.

And off we go again. This time, there's more pressure. The ball is flying everywhere. People are getting annoyed by those who aren't taking it seriously. Others are overextending, trying to go faster but messing it up. In the end, I record 35 seconds. I don't judge. I don't say anything other than, "Can you do better? "

"Yes!" Cries back a pumped-up chorus. And they're ready to go again before I have my watch set. I have to restart them because they are so eager to prove they can beat their benchmark, they jump the gun.

The next time they do improve; they get it down to 20. Everyone cheers. The person who set the goal at 20 feels vindicated. The team did it! They are almost ready to sit down when I ask again, "Can you do better? "

Some are not sure. Others say, "Darned right! Let's go!" They go again and get it down to 18.

Up to this point, they have been following the original pattern or process without questioning anything. It becomes obvious that they can only make small, incremental improvements by approaching the problem in the same way, only faster. And indeed, with more time and practice and improved skill, they can do better.

But eventually someone asks, "What are the rules again?" I respond, "Everyone has to participate and touch the ball in the same order as you established before it comes back to Tom. "

Now the wheels are turning. "Can we get into a tighter circle?," someone asks.

I nod and they all start to move to the front of the room where they can get closer without being separated by the tables. Keeners are leading the way. Others are dragging their feet wondering what the point of the game is. On the way, someone else asks, "Can we change our order so that we can just hand it off to the next person instead of tossing it across the circle?"

"Yes," I reply.

Now they are in a tight circle, standing next to the person they were once throwing to across the room, and they take the ball and pass it to the person on their left. They're down to ten seconds. I record the number.

"Can you do any better? " I ask.

"What if we all received the ball in our right hand and passed it to the next person's right hand? Some people are still touching it with both hands before passing it off and that's slowing us down." "What if every other person held their hand palm up and the others held their hand palm down? "

"What if we all just held our hands out and had Tom in the middle of the circle and he just twirls around and touches all the hands?"

"What if ?"

And before we know it, they have achieved the task in one second. What an incredible increase in performance! From 30 to one. Voices, charged with energy, are just a bit louder than before. The players are acting like they just scored a touchdown. And in a way, they have. They took a challenge and went through the steps I'm suggesting here. They measured for a benchmark, set a goal to improve, improved and measured, improved and measured, and improved. Vastly.

There are a few additional lessons that teams can learn from this exercise; that they can —

- set but also exceed a goal if they keep looking for better ways;

- spark off each other's ideas and enthusiasm to improve upon the process;

- work together as a team for higher and higher performance;

- have fun together in an improvement process;

- actually do it more easily in one second than they can in 30; and

- change the perceived rules that would hold them back, even though no one had set those rules.

The last point is critical. They could not have achieved what they did — a 3,000 percent increase in performance — if they had continued to do it the way they had in the beginning. In order to come up with a significant breakthrough in the process, they had to change what they thought were the rules. They had put up barriers for themselves that simply were not there. One time a woman even whispered to me, "Is it okay if we talk?" Of course it was; no one had told them they couldn't talk.

Then I ask them, "If I had said at the beginning that I thought you could improve your performance from 30 seconds to 1 second, how would you have responded?"

They say they would have been discouraged because it seemed to be unrealistic and unreasonable. But with just the right amount of nonjudgmental encouragement — "Can you do better" — they did it on their own. In 15 minutes, we helped them learn that processes can be examined from different angles, measured, and improved upon.

Imagine taking a similar approach with all of your important processes.

1.3 Measure again

As suggested in the above exercise, you measure, improve upon the process, and measure again to see how you're doing against the benchmark. I can almost guarantee that you will be doing better. If for some strange reason you aren't, go back to your documentation and assess what went wrong.

Create a new benchmark and level of performance that becomes the expected norm. Add checklists to the process. Get employees to fill in the checklists and make falsifying the checklist an offense warranting instant dismissal.

For this to work you have to show that you're deadly serious about it. Make it clear that if they say they cleaned the washrooms with a certain cleaner, then they better have used that cleaner. If they say they asked this question when the customer inquired about your service, then they better have asked that question. Otherwise, the system will never be as strong as it can be and you won't be able to rely on the data to make better and better decisions.

1.4 Implement

Once you feel you have the process down pat, carve it in stone. From now on, this is the way it's going to be done. Naturally, you'll continue to look for better ways, but for now you've got this process nailed and it's time to put your energies into the next one, rather than beat this one to death.

Is it going to be 100 percent perfect? Probably not, but it doesn't have to be. Even if it's 80 percent of what it could be, that's likely good enough to lock it in. It's 80 percent better than it was before.

That isn't true of systems that require absolute perfection every time, such as flight checks, security checks on pharmaceuticals, or safety checks at a nuclear plant. I'm talking about the processes that you didn't have before or those that haven't been reviewed in a long, long time, where anything is an improvement.

1.5 Measure again

You can't implement it and forget about it. You have to continue to measure and give feedback to your people to let them see that you're aware of how they are doing, and let them know that you care. Show them that the information they are gathering and comparing to the benchmark is still valuable and current — unlike the number of bicycles in the Ford parking lot.

See the downloadable forms kit for a worksheet dealing with your process.

12
TEST THE WATERS
WITH A SABBATICAL

Once you have put your processes in place and measured and improved, you should test the waters to see how well you've done. Do you have the right people in the right roles? Have you mentored and coached them sufficiently? Are they adequately trained to do their jobs? Do the company's processes run the company or is it run by the well-intentioned but unpredictable whims of the managers and employees? Can you take a vacation without checking in every day? Do you take your smart phone with you everywhere you go? Are you mentally ready to begin the process of letting go?

1. Take a Sabbatical or Long Vacation

I had some of these issues thrust upon me prematurely. I have a degenerative muscle disease: adult onset spinal muscular atrophy (SMA). In my case, it's attacked the quadriceps — those big bulky muscles in the upper legs. Well, mine used to be big and bulky, but now they're not. They are pretty much gone.

I first realized that something was wrong when I was 45, so I've lived with it now for more than 20 years. It is a syndrome that progresses slowly and there is no cure at this time. On a practical level, it means that I tire easily, have trouble with stairs, stumble or fall on uneven ground, and cannot participate in many of the sports I enjoyed when I was younger. I use a cane for support and the prognosis is that someday I will be in a wheelchair. I am doing everything I can to put that off as long as possible.

I consider this disease to be both a blessing and a curse.

The curse part is obvious. It's painful, frustrating, and sometimes discouraging.

The blessing is that it was a wake-up call for me. Like many entrepreneurs, I had always considered myself invulnerable, forever young, and capable of anything I put my mind to. I was fearless, optimistic, and the future was always bright and beautiful. In fact, the future was so bright and beautiful, I spent a lot of my time there. I was forever envisioning how great it would be when my company and I finally broke through to the other side — the huge number of people we'd help, our potential impact on the world, the financial reward, the glory, the recognition — I have always enjoyed what I do, but when I was honest with myself, I had to admit I wasn't spending enough time in the here and now. I worked my butt off for the rewards waiting for me in the future, always just around the next corner or bend in the road.

After a few years of denial, I was forced by my disease to slow down, appreciate the present, and acknowledge that there are things that are important to do now because I may not have a chance to do them in the future. I realized that many people don't get that message until it is too late. "I'll take that trip I've always dreamed of when I retire," they say, only to drop dead of a heart attack before they get around to it. I won't go so far as to say I'm thankful for my disease, but I know it could have been a lot worse. I have had the opportunity to do some things I would have otherwise put off. And for that, I am grateful.

Case in point: In 2007, my wife Dawna and I decided to plan for and take a sabbatical of six months traveling around North America in a recreational vehicle. I had a few goals that were important to me.

1. I wanted to rekindle my relationship with Dawna. We had been married for more than 30 years at that point and we weren't as close as I wished. We knew we could do better, and living together for six months in such tight quarters would

either strengthen our relationship or kill it. We figured it was better to know now, while we were both still relatively young, which way it was going to go. (And we are still married.)

2. I wanted to give the employees at my two main companies some space and a chance to run things without me overseeing them. While I had taken some of the actions I've discussed in this book, I knew I wasn't completely there yet, so this would be an excellent test to expose any cracks and determine what was still required to expand my freedom from my historically driven pace at work. There's nothing like jumping into ice-cold water to find out where the holes in your wetsuit are.

3. I wanted some time to research and begin writing this book. I wanted to meet and interview entrepreneurs in many locations who had sold their businesses whether successfully or unsuccessfully, triumphantly or with regrets. I knew that their personal experiences and what they learned through the process could benefit other business owners who were, as you are now, looking at their options.

4. With some sense of urgency, I wanted to travel and do things that I could still do that would become progressively more difficult the longer I put them off. Driving long distances was becoming painful. Simply getting in and out of our RV was hard work and any serious hiking was out of the question. Yet even with the understanding that I already had limitations, there were countless places to see and things to do that had to be undertaken and enjoyed, now or never.

We began planning our trip about a year in advance. We set a date and began to work backwards. I soon realized that there was very little literature or written advice that I could find to help us prepare for a sabbatical. We had to figure out much of this on our own.

2. The Goal

On June 1, 2007, I set a goal and put it on paper:

Dawna and I have our personal, business, and career affairs in order so that we can take six months off and travel across North America, taking a sabbatical and the time to enjoy things while I am still physically able.

Target Date: May 31, 2008

What are the benefits?

- Forces me to get focused on what's really important business-wise in the next year.
- Forces me to get mentally prepared to deal with my illness as a reality that will hamper my physical activities in the future.
- Forces me to put my health first and deal with it as proactively as possible.
- Gives my management team a chance to grow and take on more responsibility.
- Time to spend with Dawna, rekindling our relationship, doing things that we will both enjoy.
- Time to reflect on life and decide how to proceed to the next stage.
- Time to get caught up on reading and writing.
- Opportunity to write a book.
- Avoid the sense of regret I would have if I didn't do it now and couldn't later. (I have very few regrets in life and would like to keep it that way.)

What are the obstacles?

- My businesses are not ready to operate without me.
- Question of how clients, affiliates, and staff will react.
- A major program we are working on is not running yet. Needs me as a champion to get it off the ground and to develop it.
- Financial: don't know what it will cost or how we'll finance it.

Need answers to a number of questions:

- What do we do with the house?
- What do we do with the cottage?
- What do we do with the pets?
- Where do we want to travel?
- What are the best times to travel?
- What means of transportation/accommodation will we use?
- Can we do an international home exchange?
- Can I increase my physical stamina? How?

- Can I get my businesses to run without me? If so, how? Who will do it?
- Should I sell the business? Bring in a partner?
- What do I do if after taking six months off I decide I don't want to come back to the life I am currently leading, especially working so hard on my business?
- What do I do if I set up my business to run without me, or sell it, only to miss it so much that I regret doing that?
- Who can I call on to help me make these decisions in an objective, dispassionate way?
- Should we sell our cars?
- How do I maintain my energy, enthusiasm, and motivation to drive the business while planning a sabbatical for a year from now?

What are the solutions?

- Get my businesses in shape.
- Discuss plans with my managers and get buy-in.
- Put remaining procedures and processes in place.
- Identify gaps and begin to fix them.
- Increase sales and set aside some cash for my expenses.
- Mentor and coach my VP to position him to act in my place.
- Begin to talk about my plans with clients and affiliates so they are supportive and understanding.
- Write articles on what I'm doing to make it seem more normal and get others interested in taking sabbaticals as well.
- Check out costs and anticipated expenses for the time we are away and set up a bank account for putting away money.
- Make a decision on the major program. Go or no go? If I have to choose, the sabbatical will win.
- Start discussions with Dawna to determine where she would like to go.
- Contact various tourist bureaus across North America to have them send us their promotional packages.
- Check out RVs to see what it will cost and what we should expect to pay so we can negotiate the best deal.

- Get physiotherapy to establish exercises to strengthen muscles in order to be more comfortable.

- Offer the cottage to close friends and family who will take good care of it. Set up a schedule on a first-come, first-served basis.

- Get someone to rent or house-sit our home for six months.

- Get Dawna to speak to her boss.

- Identify people across North America to interview for research on the book.

From this list, I went on to develop specific action steps that are too numerous to detail here.

Dawna was cautiously happy about taking time off but needed to get permission from her employer. Because of my history as an entrepreneur, she wasn't totally convinced that I was committed to leaving my businesses behind and would in fact follow through on the date we had set. As a result, she put off asking her manager for the time off until the last minute in case I changed my mind. As it turned out, even though she was the first in her organization to ever ask for a sabbatical, her employer was quite supportive. With that hurdle cleared, we continued to work away on our list of solutions and the multiple action items that flowed from that list.

Everything seemed to fall into place. When I made the announcement at a general staff meeting that I was leaving for six months, they applauded! Now, I could have taken that two ways but I chose to believe that they were happy for me and were prepared to help. To our surprise, everyone we shared our plans with was supportive and encouraging. No one tried to dissuade us. We ended up starting our sabbatical ahead of our original target date. On March 6, 2008, we left our home and headed south. And we have no regrets. It was wonderful on many levels. It did strengthen our marriage and our relationship. It did give me time to think, plan, and reflect on my life and where I was going next. It was an incredible trip and we saw places we had only dreamed of in the past. Along the way, I met many fascinating people who had sold their businesses and openly shared their stories with me.

I did find out where the cracks were in my businesses and I fixed them as I prepared my own companies for transition.

I could tell you much more about my sabbatical (and if you're really interested and want to see pictures, send me an email). But the main message I want to share is that it is possible, that it is something you should do when you are physically able, and that it is a powerful test to see if your business is ready for sale.

3. New Possibilities

What about you? If you had six months off, what would you really, really want to do? The possibilities are endless. You could —

- volunteer overseas;

- learn to paint, take photographs, cook, fly, write poetry, surf;

- take university courses; get an Executive MBA;

- climb a mountain or a series of mountains;

- ride a bike across the continent;

- hike the West Coast Trail or the Camino de Santiago;

- live in Paris and learn French;

- start a rock band;

- spend unforgettable quality time with your children, grand-children, or parents;

- get in shape and run a marathon; or

- read the stacks of books you've bought over the years but haven't had time to open.

There's no shortage of options. The problem may be having too many options from which to choose. You may wish to go back to your roll of paper from our previous exercise — GYLOAR — to review some of the items you had there. Look at what you said was important to you in that process, then ask yourself if it would be wise or feasible to accelerate the timeline on that and bring it closer.

4. The Bucket List

If you haven't already done so, watch the movie *The Bucket List* starring Morgan Freeman and Jack Nicholson. It is as funny as it is poignant. It chronicles the final weeks of two men who meet in a cancer ward and decide to do all the things they wished they had done earlier in their lives. They sky-dive, drink expensive wine in the world's finest hotels, travel, and spend some quality family time. Their "bucket list" included all the things they wanted to do before kicking the bucket.

What's on your bucket list? If you knew you only had six months left to live, how would you choose to spend those last six months? Now ask yourself this: How do you know for sure that you do have more than six months left?

What I learned with my disease is that life is short; we can be struck with death, disability, or disaster at any time, and we absolutely must make the most of every moment. Within reason, we should do what's important to us now so that we have no regrets. Even though my businesses did not run the way I had planned or expected when I left, I have no regrets about taking the time off. None. Neither does my wife, who tends to be the more practical one in our partnership. There is no question that it was the right thing to do at that time. And if things didn't go as well in my business as I planned, then I learned from the unexpected, ascertained what needed to be improved upon, and have become a wiser, more seasoned businessperson in the process. We make mistakes and we learn our best lessons from them.

5. Time off Is Good for Your Business

I was originally inspired to take this time off by a speaker I heard at a TEC meeting. Craig, a business owner from Calgary, had realized incredible business growth in both revenues and profits and was sharing some secrets with our group.

He had complained to his business coach that he was exhausted and working ridiculous hours. When he admitted he hadn't had a holiday in years and was feeling burned out, his coach told him to book some time off for a vacation.

"I can't," Craig said. "There's just too much to do!"

His coach was adamant and insisted that Craig start with three weeks.

In spite of his misgivings, Craig agreed. He returned from his vacation with renewed energy and drive and was surprised to find that his business had actually done even better while he was away. He continued to increase his time off and eventually got everything in place to the point where he now takes three months off every year and volunteers his time overseas in a third world country.

Craig learned that while he was away, his senior management team felt more empowered to make decisions and to be accountable for the results or consequences of decisions both good and bad. They rose to the challenge and began making decisions that would have been put on Craig's desk had he been around.

He also found that when he returned, he had new business insights and creative ideas to share that he wouldn't have generated had he been in the office with his nose to the grindstone. Those ideas propelled his company to even greater heights, making his time off even more valuable to the firm than his daily labor could have ever been. Like the ball-toss game described in the previous chapter, Craig saw ways to "change the rules" that didn't actually exist in his industry but were implied in the way everyone else did business.

That's what I love about business. It's a great metaphor for life. You can't get ahead without some risk. You can't improve without trying something different. You don't always get the result you want, but you always get feedback and learn from every experience which actions you should repeat and what you should alter the next time around.

Learning to take time off and leave your business to fend without you provides an eye-opening education that you simply cannot get anywhere else, or in any other way.

6. Yeah, But ...

I can just imagine the dialogue going on in your mind as you read this:

- That's irresponsible. I would never leave people to flounder while I'm off having a good time somewhere else.

- I can't afford it. If I'm not there working, I can't justify paying myself a salary.

- Why would my employees want to work hard while I'm off enjoying myself?

- How do I track things to make sure we stay on course?

- My spouse will never agree.

- I'm not happy with my sales and profits now. What will happen if I'm not there to watch them every day?

- What will we do with the house? The kids? The cars? The pets?

- I love running my business. I can't think of anything I'd rather do right now.

- I have another 20 years to travel if I want to.

Yes, and you'll have many of the same issues when it comes time to sell your business or slow down and gradually give yourself more time off. Consider a sabbatical your trial run. I'd have to confess to having many of the same concerns ... some of them justified, as it turned out ... but I went anyway. And remember: I have no regrets. You won't, either. In their book *Six Months Off* (Holt Paperbacks, 1996), authors Dlugozima, Scott, and Sharp interviewed hundreds of people who had taken sabbaticals and did not find one person who regretted doing it. Not one!

Letting go is difficult for dyed-in-the-wool entrepreneurs. Our businesses have been our lives. But times and circumstances change, and we must take stock on an ongoing basis to see if we are still doing what makes us happy. We can become so intensely linked with our business that we fail to see everything else going on around us. Like the oblivious victim in the boiling-frog experiment, we adjust. We don't consciously register that our health is failing, our relationships have become stale, and our definition of fun is going to yet another networking event. How did we get here?

It doesn't really matter how we got here. We each took a different path. The important questions are: How do we move on? How do we let go?

See the downloadable forms kit for a worksheet dealing with your sabbatical readiness.

DOWNLOAD KIT

Please enter the URL you see in the box below into your computer web browser to access and download the kit.

www.self-counsel.com/updates/btcoach/20kit.htm

The download kit includes:

- Worksheets to help you with your transition plan
- Resources for further reading